To the memory of President John F. Kennedy

A very special

text by LAURA BERGQUIST

photographs by STANLEY TRETICK

PRESIDENT

designed by Leonard Jossel

MC GRAW-HILL BOOK COMPANY · NEW YORK · TORONTO · LONDON

CONTENTS

It would be unthinkable to dedicate this book to anyone but John F. Kennedy. Still, both the publishers and authors owe a special debt of gratitude to Mrs. John F. Kennedy, who wrote the touching tribute to her husband, quoted in these pages, for *Look* magazine's John F. Kennedy memorial issue, and also permitted the use of her picture — inscribed in a style as personal as her husband's. We owe apologies to Caroline Kennedy, for printing pictures of her at a time when her mother was doing her best to shield her from publicity and from spoiling by us vultures of the press; and a salute to John F. Kennedy, Junior, for just being himself—live-wire, talkative, natural as his father ever was.

FOREWORD

By a quirk of editorial casting, photographer Stanley Tretick and I turned out for nearly three years one story after another—daytime serial style—on the Kennedy White House for *Look* magazine.

Breezing into the White House off and on, in the line of duty, I kept an informal fever chart on that New Frontier. Generally, the prevailing mood was gay, hard-working, open-door. The youth, I must confess, was a bit unsettling. For, as columnist Mary McGrory wrote, except for the President—a senior citizen in his forties—the average age of the Administration inner circle was so tender that many citizens woke up after the inauguration to find themselves being governed largely by their juniors.

Our last close-up story of the President was the picture-text feature entitled "The President and His Son" that appeared only a few days before the Dallas nightmare. (I might add that only twice—the pictures of the golf cart and JFK with his son—did we ever show the President any *Look* pictures in advance, and never words.)

Stanley had proudly trotted over to the White House with an advance *Look* issue to show off his handiwork on the JFK, Jr. story. It was one of those hectic Presidential days, and after some waiting, Tretick said to Mrs. Lincoln perhaps he'd just leave the issue. No, she said in her motherly fashion, she knew how long and doggedly Tretick had worked to pry that story loose from the White House; he deserved to present it to the President personally.

JFK leafed through the issue, muttering words of approval about the photographs—he loved those pictures of his son. Nearly always he had some comment to make about any story you did, no matter what the subject, in or out of the White House. (Once after I'd done a lighthearted piece on Caroline, he mildly criticized: "You know, she's not all that smart.")

What was grand and startling about this President was that he didn't forget journalists who'd known him when: Stanley had first met up with him on the Presidential campaign, as the photographer who'd traveled the most miles on that extraordinary ordeal. In '57, in the course of doing a story on "The Brothers Kennedy," I had trailed Senator Kennedy and Ted Sorensen through several states when he seemed to be questing hopelessly (to me) for the Presidency.

Tretick and I had one thing in common; an endless curiosity about John F. Kennedy. We were not true gung-ho idolators—indeed like many citizens who feel free to quarrel with Chief Executives, I often took issue with his policy. We were not even White House "regulars," nor old journalist friends, like Ben Bradlee or Charlie Bartlett, who were often invited to dine at the White House. We just dug JFK. When friends accused me of having become a Kennedy "fink," my defense was that whatever you thought of his politics, John F. Kennedy was a totally "fascinating human animal." For lack of a better adjective, Tretick and I would fall back on describing him as "nifty"—a man candid, straight, great to work with, wickedly funny and enormously bright. His Irish temper might boil on occasion—once we were objects of his wrath—but there was never anything mean or vindictive or pretentious or boring about him. Whether he was a great President or not, or had the potential for becoming one, I leave to historians and scholars. For us, he was a *nifty* human being.

What he knew about your own business was discouraging. He knew, for example, exactly what *Look's* "lead" time (i.e., deadline) was, when I had forgotten it. Once, he startled *Look* editorial director Dan Mich by remarking he'd just scanned the latest magazine circulation figures and noted that *Look's* readership was then ahead of a certain nameless competitor.

As a President, and subject, he commanded critical respect, rather than awe; there you sat, talking, as if to a friendly contemporary, about Cuba or Dorothy Kilgallen—subjects serious or otherwise. What was amazing, was that people around the world felt that way about him, too. Often in my travels in Latin America, young Latin leftists, endemically anti-Yanqui, on hearing I covered the White House would urge me to explain some problem or other to Kennedy, sure he'd understand or at least listen. Even that most extreme anti-American, Cuban guerilla warfare expert Ernesto "Che" Guevara, on his trip to New York, confided that of all the Americans he'd like to meet most now, it would be Jacqueline Kennedy. Harold Macmillan, former prime minister of Great Britain, has said in his forthcoming memoirs that he not only liked John F. Kennedy, but came to love him. Not until November 22 did even I realize that I had such deep affection for this complex, open, and elusive man.

I can imagine him scanning this volume with expert editorial eye, a thought capable of making you nervous, approving some pictures here, taking exception to words there. It is the personal record of two journalists who covered that short-lived New Frontier, and many thanks go to the editors of *Look* magazine for opening up the rich files of Stanley Tretick's photo reportage for publication. Thanks, too, to editor Daniel D. Mich, who also often visited the Kennedy White House on *Look* business and was as beguiled by the goings-on there as we were. The words are culled from dozens of my old notebooks, jam-packed with Kennedy-iana, plus Stanley Tretick's tape, and record of his adventures on the campaign, for the Kennedy library.

Many thanks, too, to Leonard Jossel, most gifted of art directors, for the book's handsome design, and his hard-working assistant Joe Knox; and double gratitude to novelist and *Look* writer Fletcher Knebel, who, as an ex-member of the Cowles' Washington bureau, did many Kennedy stories himself and helped straighten out my tangled prose.

Thanks most of all to John F. Kennedy, his family, and New Frontiersmen for providing two journalists with some of the most stimulating material of a lifetime. Somehow, even writing about John F. Kennedy in the past tense seems wrong—how can that terribly alive, electric, ever-changing and growing human being be gone from our lives?

A
very special
President

Through 1,036 days of the New Frontier, from its take-off in a bracing Washington blizzard, to its sudden, crumpled end on that bright Dallas day, lived a very special President—a dispassionate intellectual, self-deprecating wit, sailor, reader of poetry, fastidious dresser, tribal-devoted father, a man of grace, charm, and elegance.

The 170-year-old Presidency had never known another like him. To the traditionally dreary precinct of politics he brought zest, flair, a style (that much overworked word). There was his abundance of youth; his thatch of chestnut hair, the wealth—and the built-in confidence which comes of it—his crackling mind; his trim, lean figure; his wispy, flicking smile; his almost frigid restraint under pressure. He admired science. (Though he had no love for the "dismal science" of economics, he applied his hungry mind to its conquest.) He was a qualified patron of the arts. He courted excellence in all its forms. He was a word man who wrote well before he became a politician. He painted semi-well. He read voraciously and swiftly. He lived with pain. He never flinched at danger. He was cool under duress, but he wept when his infant son Patrick died. He swam, he sailed, he danced. His enthusiasms, though leashed, were many and diverse. "Life piled on life was all too little for him," wrote his wife in the summer of 1964. "He lived at such a pace because he wanted to know it all." His mind stored facts like a computer. He could be tart, brittle, withdrawn at times. At other moments, he could open the doors of the heart with a bright, boyish, Irish smile.

He was, in short, the pride of western civilized man. The sum of him inspired a John F. Kennedy cult incredible in its proportions and extent, from the bogs of Ireland to the mud-hut villages of Africa. From Mexico City to Bangkok his name still is magic. People in remote lands who can neither read nor write can remember precisely where they were and what they were doing at the moment of his death. "I feel suddenly old without Mr. and Mrs. Kennedy in the White House," wrote a Harvard master. "Not only by ability, but by sheer verve and joy, the Kennedys imparted their youth to everyone and put a sheen on our life that made it more youthful than it is . . . now it is August, not June."

He was a bright, racing star who lighted men's thoughts and their dreams, though who could know that at the time? No one would have been more astonished than this complex fascinating man, who rarely voiced in public the deep passions he felt about events, who worried that he "wasn't getting his message across," to find that he was not only admired all over the world, but loved.

His time was but a flash in history; he said in his inaugural message his hopes wouldn't be fulfilled in the first 1,000 days, not even perhaps "in our lifetime" on this planet, and he scarcely got more than a thousand. Historians must judge him now, though he brought to that office far more than the "style" belabored in the eulogies—qualities of courage, rationality, and spaciousness into American life.

To many of us who covered him at the White House, he was a wry contemporary, a man who talked one's own language, knew all the inside jokes, read omnivorously, and often seemed the easiest man to see in Washington on short notice. The appointment schedule might shift, perhaps on the day the Russians resumed nuclear testing, but still Himself could be seen. The best time of day was 6 P.M. onward, a time when he unwound with old friends or newspaper callers. Whether long or short, these were tumbling sessions that left the caller breathless as if one were racing a long-distance runner. If a new novel, still unpublished, was recommended to him, he'd already read it. If a snide crack in a Broadway gossip column was mentioned, he'd heard about it. If he was told, somewhat sheepishly, that a profile of his three-year-old daughter, Caroline, was being written, he would offer to help make it an "authorized" biography.

He was always exhilarating, but often *unsettling*. For Presidents up to his time had seemed another breed; grandfatherly, Olympian, remote, such as Eisenhower, who inflicted a certain stuffiness on the capital city. Or for a generation of New Deal causemongers, Franklin Roosevelt had been the seemingly permanent idol. Now, suddenly running the country from the White House, was this hip, unstarchy, ferociously candid Irish intellectual who had broken every rule in the political book to get where he was. Granted that he was light-years brighter, more disciplined, more certain of his destiny than others of his generation, still he was of that new generation with all its qualms and perplexities. His was a generation of promise, but one unproved in the executive suites or on the stage of world politics. Writer Murray Kempton, musing on JFK's relationship to his generation, saw the President as the kid in the class who was better than his mates, but inspired no envy.

When Jack Kennedy moved into the old mansion on Pennsylvania Avenue, it became a swinging White House, so loose and wide-open in the early days that one felt, while prowling its corridors, a bit like Eliza Doolittle let loose in Buckingham Palace. "Seeing the Tiger?" a staffer would inquire casually on meeting in the West Wing. That set the tone of the entire establishment, an admiring but never a reverential tone. Secretaries first-named their bosses. African heads of states in helicopters rained steadily on the South Lawn. No chief of an emerging nation was anybody until he had his picture taken with JFK. Caroline used the lawn with her playmates, rolling downhill in barrels or bickering with the ducks in the fountain. At night were the sparkling late dinner dances, where the "in" crowd danced to the music of Lester Lanin. To the mansion came a sheen, a cluttered brilliance. Washington suddenly eclipsed Hollywood as the nation's glamour capital, causing Betty Beale, queen bee society reporter for the Washington *Star,* to fret that New York editors were discovering her town as if it were "Togoland or some quaint place equally unknown."

All this was heady stuff for the working journalist, chiefly because he was welcomed to the fold. Even a writer who had known Senator Kennedy fleetingly in the early 50's would not be overlooked. The President did not forget those who Knew Him When.

In a world ruled by old men, Kennedy was a leader born in the twentieth century—and well into that century. A new generation, a new outlook, a new style had taken over, and many Americans realized shakily that this generation was their own. That made them nervous, knowing how fallible they were.

Some callers did not feel at all comfortable in this personalized White House which so reflected the complex, prismatic man in the Oval Office. Graying New Dealers, nostalgic for FDR, would complain that they didn't vibrate on the same wave length with this cool, quizzical pragmatist. Where, they asked, was the charisma, the passion, the conviction?

Arthur Krock, senior *New York Times* pundit, once took an avuncular swipe at JFK whom he'd known as a boy. By inviting newsmen and publishers to lunch, scolded Krock, the new President was blurring their critical faculties with his charm. But it wasn't the charm that made this man a special President, nor the romantic cliché that he was a storybook President, with a beautiful wife at his side. No, it was much more than that. No matter what marks history might give him for statecraft, Jack Kennedy was a completely fascinating human animal.

He didn't seem to stir the emotions at first so much as the mind. Still many of us working journalists around the mansion felt a proprietary interest in the White House. If JFK pulled a scorching blunder, such as the Bay of Pigs, we despaired. If he did something splendid on civil rights, we might cheer him with a personal note. For a man stereotyped as "cool," an adjective which irritated his wife, Kennedy provoked a curious kind of involvement in others. He was the President always, but at the same time one of us, an insider. Landing in Paris, on that triumphal tour with Jackie, he turned to the press regulars and gave them a little, low wave of the hand as if to say: "Well, buddies, we're all in this together, and isn't it grand?" Once during the nerve-shattering week of the Cuban missile crisis, a photographer doggedly waited, day in and day out, to snap JFK with other members of "Excom," the small band that weathered the ordeal with him. "Boy, I've really sweated it out this week," the cameraman said to Kennedy. "Just what do you think I've been doing?" came the reply.

4

It became the fashion to write about the style of this youngest President ever—the class, the grace, the presence, the aplomb under duress. These engaging qualities were soon widely imitated among young government officials in Washington, but what beguiled observers more was the curiosity of the man, the way the wheels spun around in his head. He was one of the nosiest humans ever, not in the sense of a snooper or pryer, but in the manner of the great reporters and novelists. He was omnicurious about everything, books, people, ideas, romances, policies, cults. Perhaps it was the ex-newsman in him, perhaps the Harvard student but he just had to *know* everything.

Records of the Pablo Casals concert in the White House had a phenomenal sale, but he wanted to know exactly how many had been sold. As he talked with a caller in the Oval Office, he'd suddenly jump up and stroll across the room and peer through the French doors opening on the Rose Garden which was being replanted and redesigned under his wife's direction. He checked daily on the progress of the renovation. "Struck oil yet?" he called out to the men digging and planting.

Doing what came naturally, driving a golf cart, playing with his son John, immersed in talk with a group of Peace Corps recruits, he was no problem for photographers. He ignored the cameras. But in formal portraits he often looked as stiff as a department store dummy. During one especially trying camera session in the oval living room of the family quarters, he sat on a spindle-legged chair, feet curled around the legs. He was visibly impatient and restless, coming to life only when he looked up and said: "Say, have you read the new Herbert Matthews' book on Cuba?" The caller discovered she had, for the first time, read a book before the President. A lively discussion about Matthews' opinions kept Kennedy pinned to the chair for a full five minutes, while the photographer worked.

His curiosity had no artificial limits. For instance, he loved the tinkle of personal, small talk about him. His No. 2 secretary was twenty-one-year-old Priscilla Wear, otherwise known as "Fiddle." Fresh out of Goucher College and fascinated by politics, she volunteered to work on the campaign, and wound up assisting Mrs. Evelyn Lincoln, the President's personal secretary. Fiddle was a delightful, bright girl, funny and vague. She amused the President with her breathless, artless gossip about small doings in the outside world. Her talents as a secretary were, to put it mildly, minor. She typed a bit, scrawled the Presidential autographs, and helped answer the phones. When she and her side-kick roommate, "Faddle," Jill Cowen, twenty-three, who did odd jobs for Press Secretary Pierre Salinger, threw parties in their Georgetown houses (they moved every few months), the top echelon of the New Frontier dropped by to dance the limbo until 3 A.M. Still she fretted that she wasn't getting anywhere, careerwise—and that

from a girl who worked at the very power center of the world. Once, seriously, she asked JFK if, to improve herself, she shouldn't take a shorthand course. "What's the matter," he asked, "you getting ambitious?"

Let a love affair bloom overnight in the White House circle and JFK knew about it. When one of the prettier White House reporters was interviewing him one day for a solemn news story, he startled her by asking: "How's your romance going?" Around the press room it was common knowledge that she was enamored of a fellow journalist not yet legally untangled from his wife. "Well," she replied, "there are problems. You know he's still married." "Is that a fact," the President spoofed. "Aren't we all?"

Producer Otto Preminger burst on the town like a Prussian Cecil B. De Mille to film the political spectacular, "Advise and Consent." His mammoth cast included the President's brother-in-law, Peter Lawford, Fiddle and Faddle, Senators, newsmen, and even the Sheraton Park Hotel doorman. A big party scene was being filmed one night at a Washington estate when the phone rang. It was JFK calling Peter Lawford to check on how things were going. "He's dying to be here," said one associate. "He can't stand to be left out of anything."

Even after the inaugural binge wore off and crises began to batter in earnest, there was a great sense of fun in that White House. "You couldn't wait to get to work in the morning," a secretary recalls, "to see what would happen. People worked hard, they certainly realized the seriousness of what they were doing and the responsibility they had, but they didn't take *themselves* seriously." Curiously, President Eisenhower once said that was the way to run a government. But in JFK's time, the theory became a gay reality.

Visiting the JFK White House regularly was like attending a cliff-hanging serial movie. One wondered what would happen in the next installment. Emperor Haile Selassie paid a state visit, and young John, fresh from his bath, wandered in, stark naked, to greet the monarch. When Secretary of the Treasury Douglas Dillon flew back from the Inter-American Conference in Punta del Este, where he had helped to launch the Alliance for Progress and dueled verbally with the Cuban antagonist, Commandante Ernesto "Che" Guevara, the President threw an impromptu champagne party and supper in the family living quarters for Dillon. Young Jim Symington, son of the Senator from Missouri, brought along his guitar and plunked out a new folk song he'd concocted for the occasion, "Alianza y Progreso," singing with a foot propped on one of Mrs. Kennedy's delicate French chairs. In the office of that youthful Gray Eminence, Ted Sorensen, whom JFK once called his "intellectual blood bank," a top hat hung on the hat tree. Whatever for? He'd worn it at the Inauguration, said this Nebraska boy, and "it's the only top hat I've ever worn or ever will."

Nothing was too trivial for the bounding Presidential imagination.

Once Bill Walton, the politico-artist friend of both Kennedys, casually mentioned that the trash baskets near the Washington Monument were old-fashioned eye sores. Well then, said JFK, let's get someone to design new ones. Raymond Loewy did. It appeared briefly that the old buildings circling Lafayette Square, the park which fronted the White House, would be razed to make way for glittering, modern executive offices —until the President got in the act. Walton would bring over new models, which JFK studied while working out with dumbbells in the White House gym. "I don't want any Williamsburg," he said, overriding his wife's preference for a Georgian design. He settled for a mixture of modern buildings set behind the best preserved of the old houses.

The difference between the Eisenhower and Kennedy eras, one old Washington hand remarked, was that between a slow march and a jig. In the first 100 days, while the euphoria of the Inauguration still hung in the air, an astonishing variety of people streamed through the Oval Office; Harry Truman, beauty queens, 4-H members, Baptists, award winners. If they were bona fide celebrities, the President often took them through the press office, chiefly because he felt the secretaries would get a charge out of seeing the famous. The long working day was the vogue, but once on a fall day, no one seemed to be around. The World Series was on, the President had money in the baseball pool, and, following his lead, everyone was glued to the TV set.

There was a whole new insider's lingo. The Tiger was JFK. The Thinking Machine was Secretary of Defense Robert S. McNamara. The Smiling Irishman was Dave Powers, old Boston pal, special assistant to the President, unofficial court jester, and premier baseball statistician. The President's Batman was John J. "Muggsy" O'Leary, a salty, near-toothless Irishman who used to get Senator Kennedy to the planes on time and now had a vague job in the Secret Service, a duty which included taking Caroline out to play in distant parks. The "in" ploys were numerous, but one of the most inward was that of Mrs. Leonard Bernstein, wife of the conductor. At one of Mrs. Kennedy's splendid do's, honoring composer Igor Stravinsky's upcoming eightieth birthday, Mrs. Bernstein turned to Madame Stravinsky as the ladies adjourned after dinner: "I should take your wrap, Vera, dear. It's very chilly in the Red Room."

Kennedy-dropping became a major Washington sport, which had to be played subtly. There were so many of them and they were so friendly. If one didn't know Jackie, at least Ethel would always say hi. Master at the game of inside Kennedy-dropping was a television reporter who mentioned casually in Hyannis that he'd been out golfing that day, using the President's clubs. Bobby-dropping was fair sport, but Salinger-dropping was too easy and didn't count.

The New York Times was read down to the last line of Arthur Krock,

even by White House secretaries. They never knew when the President might ask had one read that particular paragraph in such-and-such a column this morning. "I'd rather be Krocked than Fleesonized," JFK once cracked, confessing that columnist Doris Fleeson's barbs occasionally got under his skin. If action was in style, so was culture. Labor Secretary Arthur Goldberg, settling the Metropolitan Opera strike, opened a press conference by reading a grateful wire from singer Leontyne Price who said she was sending him Bach's "Goldberg Variations." After debating Khrushchev's son-in-law, Alexsei Adzhubei, on a New York TV show, Salinger invited him, in impromptu fashion, down to Washington for a backyard barbecue at his Lake Barcroft home—and next day borrowed the No. 2 President yacht, the *Patrick J.*, to take him cruising on the Potomac.

The youth of the new establishment upset the older, crusted layers of Washington's political structure. At forty-three, the President often seemed the elder statesman of the White House. Once at a New Frontier party at the home of Welfare Secretary Abraham Ribicoff, prior to a Carl Sandburg reading in the State Department, one correspondent was stunned to find herself almost the oldest person in the room. There was Sorensen, the speech-writing pundit at age thirty-three, and Dick Goodwin, specialist advisor on Latin American affairs, still in his twenties. The correspondent confessed her unease to Willard Wirtz, then Under Secretary of Labor. Wirtz grinned. "Don't worry," he said, "I'm almost fifty."

The youth of the Administration was a target for political foes. Congressman Bruce Alger, Texas Republican, took a whack at Salinger as a "young and inexperienced White House publicity man," and questioned the wisdom of having him visit the Soviet Union. "I wonder," asked a reporter at a Presidential press conference, "if you have any comments." JFK fielded the question handily: "I know there are always some people who feel that Americans are always young and inexperienced, and foreigners are always able and tough and great negotiators. But I don't think the United States would have acquired its present position of leadership in the free world if that view were correct. Now he [Alger] . . . also said that Mr. Salinger's main job was to increase my standing in the Gallup poll. Having done that, he is now moving on [laughter] to improve our communications. . . . I don't think we should worry so much about Americans traveling abroad. I think they've acquitted themselves well and so will Mr. Salinger. I'm sure that some people in the Soviet Union are concerned about Mr. Adzhubei's visits abroad."

(But JFK was not quite as insouciant about the criticism of Pierre's mission to Moscow as he seemed. Photographer Stanley Tretick and I trailed Pierre to Moscow and when we caught up with him in the U.S. Embassy, after he'd spent a day skeet-shooting at Khrushchev's country dacha, he waved us away with a White House cable. It was signed by McGeorge Bundy, the Harvard prof turned foreign policy specialist, but sent at the direction of the President who had learned of our trip. The White House dictum: At all odds, avoid the *Look* writer-photographer team.)

Any conversation with the President could take dizzy, unexpected detours. There was the time, for instance, when I broached him and his assistants on the possibility of a whole magazine issue devoted to the New Frontier's new pace in Washington. The idea was to sound him out personally, for he was the best sparker of editorial ideas in his own White House. He sent word that he would be interested in discussing the project, so one noon in August, 1961, I was put down on the Presidential appointment list.

In Mrs. Lincoln's inner office, I could see through the open door that the President's Oval Room was jammed with the top brass of the U.S. government. Mrs. Lincoln apologized profusely. It was an emergency, she explained, and the appointment would have to be postponed until later in the day. The guard at the White House gate, commiserating, speculated that they were probably commemorating a new postage stamp. Only in the next morning's newspapers did one learn the reason for the powwow of the brass: the Russians had resumed nuclear testing.

On such days, when the White House crackled with deadly serious activity, a caller felt guilty about being there at all. Still, I returned about 4 P.M. and waited in the Fish Room, so named when FDR installed a tropical fish tank there. Now a stuffed sailfish caught by Kennedy on his Acapulco honeymoon adorned a wall. A preoccupied Bobby Kennedy came trekking through, along with an assortment of V.I.P.s. The fellow waiters in the Fish Room included an impressively beribboned General Bruce Clarke, who said he'd just flown in from Berlin to report to the President on the latest crisis there. I vowed to get in and out quickly, assuaging the guilt feeling about wasting a President's time on such a day.

A certain paralysis normally hits the Presidential visitor upon entering the Oval Office, but it was more acute this time. Kennedy was his most "tan, fit and confident" self, to quote Dave Powers' favorite descriptive phrase, and he talked engagingly about the prospective magazine issue. Thirty minutes went by, then forty. Each time I ventured a lame and elaborate leave-taking remark, he interrupted with more talk. He talked on—and on. He hoped the articles wouldn't concentrate on the White House alone. That was getting enough publicity, he said. What about coverage on Capitol Hill? There was a fresh, interesting personality up there, Congressman Richard Bolling, a Missouri Democrat. Why not explore him, suggested the President. This in itself was intriguing editorial guidance from the Democratic party leader. Veteran House Speaker Sam Rayburn

was ailing and a struggle was shaping up for the majority leadership. Carl Albert of Oklahoma, then the party whip, was to be the winner, but it was obvious that Bolling was the Presidential favorite.

Then, suddenly, in the midst of politics came one of those unexpected Kennedy conversational switches that could so unsettle a caller. "Heard that the people in the Washington Cowles bureau," he said, "have been calling around the country about my 'secret' marriage." The "secret marriage" was the hottest undercover rumor running wild through the capital and the country. Dozens of newsmen had been doing detective work, trying to prove or disprove JFK's alleged marriage to a certain Durie Malcolm, now Mrs. Thomas Shevlin of Palm Beach and Newport society. The rumor had been born from a tiny, obscure entry in a Blauvelt family genealogy which someone had spotted in Washington's D.A.R. library. The President knew, though his caller didn't, that a Cowles reporter had put in an exploratory call to a St. Louis lawyer who handled Mrs. Shevlin's second divorce. The news of that call, it turned out later, had winged back to the White House with the speed of light. The lawyer had phoned Robert Kennedy who quickly called JFK. Since Kennedy himself had brought up the subject, he was asked whether he admitted to knowing the lady at all? Oh, he said, he'd taken her out a few times in the late 40's. As a young bachelor, newly elected to Congress, he'd squired her to an Orange Bowl game in Miami. But that was it, he said, except for the fact that the Shevlins and the Kennedys were friendly socially. He bantered about the "secret" marriage rumor, but in his final remark on the subject he meant business: "You print that story and I just might wind up owning *Look* magazine." The message was loud and clear. There was to be no printing of this unconfirmed, perhaps libelous, rumor about this President. Since the President seemed in the mood for chit-chat, one more question could be chanced. Did he intend one day to write his Presidential memoirs? Yes, he might, he replied. But, speaking practically, might not they be worth more if he was in office two terms?

These darting, acrobatic shifts of his mind left a caller thoroughly shook up. One might talk to him about Jackie, but abruptly he was picking the visitor's brains about Fidel Castro. The subject might start with Caroline, but soon it might switch to "Che" Guevara. The Presidential mood varied widely. Some days he was preoccupied and withdrawn. Other times the talk was utterly serious with no detours. He had a message to get across. Then there were the buoyant, erratic, gossipy days. Ted Sorensen once spelled it out like this: "He's exuberant at times. He's discouraged at times. There are events which interest him and those which bore him. There are those things which make him laugh and there are those which make him sad. And nothing is done by anyone else to dispel them, I suppose."

He changed and sobered with the months, of course, as all Presidents must. On January 20, 1961, as one President watcher said, Kennedy plunged into the Presidency with so much relish he seemed bent not only on being his own Secretaries of State and Defense but his own Mrs. Roosevelt as well. A curious elation gripped Washington, a fresh feeling that perhaps the nation's huge problems were soluble after all, if tackled with youth, strength, and vigor. January 20, Ted Sorensen remarked, had been Kennedy's "moment of glory. Everyone had told him he didn't have a chance, and now he had reached the No. 1 power center." But after that heady beginning, the first year seemed anticlimactic to many critics. JFK wooed the neutrals, only to find them at Belgrade more concerned about the approval of the Russians. Money was wrested from Congress for an accelerated arms race and a dash to the moon, but not for education. Staffers said he was a far more "humble" man than the cocksure young candidate who had debated Richard M. Nixon like a brainy statistician. He was more philosophic, they said, more aware that the President of the United States couldn't solve all the world's problems.

The fate of the 1,200 Cuban invaders at the Bay of Pigs sobered him. So did the cold bath encounter with Khrushchev in Vienna. In a speech on a West Coast swing, his longest political junket since the Inaugural, he said: "We must face the fact that the United States is neither omnipotent nor omniscient, that we are only 6 per cent of the world's population, and that we can not right every wrong or reverse each adversity, and that therefore there can not be an American solution for every world problem."

To publisher Gardner Cowles, at a White House gala, he stated the same thought in personal terms: "If a man stays in hot politics long enough, he acquires an albatross. Dick Nixon has Goody Knight [who was giving Nixon trouble in his race for governor of California]. I've got Cuba." Indeed, Cuba was an obsession with him that first year. In many conversations, even casual ones, he'd mention his "albatross."

In his rocking chair in the Oval Office one gray fall day, he mused about the Presidency and the problems of his first year. In a way, he said, he was leading a more tranquil life. "For four years," he said, "my life was far more exhausting than it is now. Remember, just before the White House, I'd gone into seven primaries, and it was a terrible physical grind." Yes, he added, all those visits by Foreign Somebodies were a drain on time and energy, but there was a distinct policy advantage in face-to-face meetings. If the President talked to a Nehru personally, if he became familiar with a man, it helped in future dealings with him. But still, he asked indignantly, how did one cope with a character like ex-President Janios Quadros of Brazil? He had tried to respect his stance as a neutral, he played it straight with him, and then Quadros ups and resigns his job in a huff, taking a few parting whacks at the United States.

Americans, he ruminated, hadn't fully fathomed how much the world had changed. "The United States," he said, "has been accustomed to so much influence we've become heavily involved in areas where our will can't be exercised. What people don't realize is that just nuclear superiority in weapons isn't a magical safeguard any more. We can't be the international gendarme for the world. We're overextended as it is. Besides, when you get right down to it, Americans don't much want to fight in exotic, far-off places like Southeast Asia."

In some ways, he said, the Russians had it easier—for all the wrong reasons. Suddenly their space program convinced people all over the world that the Russians were ahead, that their system was superior. "All the evidence shows," he said, "that in essentials we're way ahead. Russian housing is lousy, their food and agricultural system is a disaster, but those facts aren't publicized. Suddenly we're competing in a race for space we didn't even realize we were in. No matter what progress you make, the critics bomb away that we're second in space."

Yes, some criticism irritated him. It was said that he wasn't "getting across to the people," that he should make more fireside chats to the country à la FDR. James Reston, he noted, had started it in his *New York Times* column. Let one columnist or reporter sound a theme, observed the President, and the journalist imitators took up the same idea. That was a helluva way for newsmen to operate. No, it didn't bother him, being tagged with the label, "pragmatic." "At least," he said: "We do things that work."

Then, jumping up, he rummaged through his desk and came up with a sheet of figures. Did you know, he asked, that FDR gave only four fireside chats in his first year, that some years he didn't give any at all, that the average over thirteen years was only three a year? The drafting of a good speech, he said, took hours from at least three days of working time, for himself and key staffers. Was it worth it? And if a President sounded an alarm every few weeks, who'd listen any more?

One tough job of the Presidency, he went on, never made headlines. It was the task of recruiting able men for secondary jobs. Where did you find good men who can speak Spanish for ambassadorial posts in Latin America? How can you convince a top-rank executive to take a post in a federal regulatory commission?

Finally, he was asked the kind of corny question which he liked the least, but which always interested ordinary mortals. What was it like to be the President of the United States? What were the rewards, the disappointments? Had it become, as some students of the Presidency said, an impossible job? The candor ceased. The encyclopedic reeling off of facts and figures ended. The New England reticence took over. He thought for a few seconds, rocked in his chair, massaged his ankle, fingered his tie. His left hand flicked at his chest beneath his coat, while his right hand drummed on the arm of the rocker.

"Let's go on to another question," he said. "I'm not very good at that couch talk."

But the sober, reflective Kennedy is not the President that the mind recalls. Instead one pictures the taut ebullience, the lively brain, the darting curiosity. The frankness was startling. Reporters often could have destroyed him with just one off-the-record remark, but somehow no one ever did. "You been around Stevenson much?" he asked one newsman before the Democratic convention of 1960. "What's your feeling about him?" The reporter vacillated. Well, said JFK, Adlai Stevenson seemed "all right when he had a bunch of dowagers around him," but with men he somehow "didn't know how to act" at times.

"Those who know and like him tend to tell him everything," a novelist friend once said of Kennedy. "You feel he ought to know and he's terribly interested." Staffers frequently urged newspaper people to relay their findings and judgments to the President. Once, talking to Sorensen, a reporter fretted that some of the President's friends were not helping to burnish his image in Latin America at a time when he was trying to launch the Alliance for Progress. For example, Senator George Smathers of Florida, a close friend of the President, seemed to turn up too often on the side of those opposing reforms. He was an apologist for Dictator Trujillo in the Dominican Republic, for one thing. Of course, old friendships didn't influence White House policy, but the Latins didn't know that. "Tell that to the President," urged Sorensen. Who me? was the reply. "Sure," said Ted. "You're an outsider, you've no ax to grind. He'll listen to you." Perhaps nothing the casual observer said to the President actually influenced policy, but the informant knew that JFK tucked the most astonishing assortment of facts away in that remarkable mind.

His knowledge about strangers constantly amazed them. Once David Douglas Duncan, an artist of a photographer who had done a superb picture-text book on the Kremlin, was negotiating to photograph Mrs. Kennedy's refurbishing of the White House. He was waiting his turn in the press lobby when, suddenly, out from the Fish Room, strode President Kennedy with President Goulart of Brazil in tow. They headed for the doorstep which was swarming with newsreel and TV men. A veteran White House photographer asked Duncan if he'd like to meet Kennedy. "Of course," he replied, protesting that you just don't buttonhole a President. Sure you do, was the reply, and as Kennedy re-entered the lobby, the White House regular touched the President's elbow and introduced Duncan. Of course, Kennedy knew all about Duncan's proposed project and thought it would make a "terrific" book. "That was an excellent job on the Kremlin," he added. "Fascinating anecdotes." Then, to Duncan's amazement, Kennedy mentioned a specific episode in the book.

Blarneying with pompous Congressmen bored Kennedy, but he seemed to have an elastic calendar for off-beat palaver with foreign students, Peace Corps recruits, foreign heads of states, writers, whoever piqued his interest. "You looking for me?" he'd call out to a staffer who just happened to be passing in the corridor outside his office. Pamela Turnure, Mrs. K's press secretary, says that she knew hell must be breaking loose in the West Wing, if she'd get a spate of calls from the President. Just what, he wanted to know, was the seating arrangement for the State Dinner, who was sitting next to whom? What about those fireworks for the King of Afghanistan? How long would they last? No more than five minutes, he hoped, because they might disturb the peaceful slumbers of his civil servants. Did she know that she had to get permission from the District of Columbia to fire them off? Were they American or Japanese made?

That insatiable curiosity kept everyone off balance. The door between his office and that of Mrs. Lincoln was invariably open, except when some confidential matter of national security was being discussed. Once, when a reporter chatted with Mrs. Lincoln, the President burst out and began to riffle the papers on her desk. Mrs. Lincoln saved articles that might whet his interest, but nine times out of ten he had already read them. "Hi," he said this time. "Read your piece on the Dominican Republic. Whatever happened to that dwarf?" This intelligence was incredible, for in thousands of words about the neurotic post-Trujillo republic, there had been one sentence about "Snowball," a dwarf who specialized in exotic tortures. Was it true, asked Kennedy, that so many VIP Americans had been playing Dictator Trujillo's game? Yes, he was told (although he already knew it), including some friends of his. Porfirio Rubirosa, long-time Trujillo henchman, had been a weekend guest at the Kennedy compound at Hyannis at the very time when both the Dominican Republic and Cuba were outlawed from the Organization of American States. "Let's talk about it sometime," said the President and trotted back into his office.

These impromptu encounters were unsettling because his curiosity often provoked brash answers to the President's abrupt questions. Only later did the caller sweat over the gratuitous offerings. But JFK loved the give-and-take, and prided himself on being able to take it as well as dish it out. He needled constantly, intentionally confusing one writer's work with another, spotting a personality foible or twitting a person about a change in attitude. Once I noticed a society column note, saying that Kennedy's brother-in-law, Stephen Smith, had been seen dining with Rubirosa in New York. I dashed off an impulsive note to Smith, saying shame, shame, shame for associating with the likes of such a Trujillo handyman.

Smith told JFK, who instructed him in the proper response: Just tell her shame, shame, shame for associating with the likes of Che Guevara, the Cuban revolutionary whom the writer had interviewed.

JFK always thought newspaper folk needed educating. If a writer were bound for Cuba, he'd recommend some excellent dispatches in the London *Times* by Henry Brandon. He urged the reading of books, articles, and profiles. He did the same with associates and cabinet officers. His rapid reading ability, up to 3,000 words a minute, enabled him to gobble up the printed word. Once, swapping book notes, a caller suggested that he read *Seven Days in May,* a political novel about a take-over of the U.S. Government in a future military coup. Although the book was still in galley proofs, Kennedy already had read it and, of course, pondered its theme. He even ticked off specific names of some generals at the Pentagon whom he thought might hanker to duplicate fiction.

He was ever the editorial helpmate. Once, I was working on a profile of his brother-in-law, Steve Smith, my umpteenth New Frontier topic. Smith obviously was going to play a key role in the 1964 re-election campaign. It was a hectic Presidential day when I called to discuss the piece. A group of rabbis were just departing as I entered the Oval Office. "How is the piece going?" Kennedy asked. Tough, I replied. Smith was so cool, contained, and nonrevelatory that Democrats had dubbed him "the Mona Lisa of the administration." "Well, now," suggested JFK, the helpful collaborator, "why not play the story that way? I've got an idea for your lead, a quote about President Martin Van Buren which fits Steve perfectly: 'He rowed to his objective on silent oars.'"

I brought up some complaints by liberal Democratic senators, facing re-election fights, that the Kennedy election team seemed to favor party regulars in the big cities who could deliver the vote. Reformers were getting the cold shoulder, they complained. His pale eyebrows narrowed. "Hell," he exploded, "has that crybaby Senator so-and-so been complaining to you?" It was not the job of the National Committee or the White House, he said acidly, to settle every local factional fight. And then, abruptly, one of those weird conversational detours. What did I know about the gold flow?

Gold flow? Gold flow? I knew vaguely that it was a nagging economic problem, that too much Fort Knox bullion had been escaping the country, but I confessed I couldn't balance my own check book, much less fathom the esoterics of international finance. That was *his* problem, he mused: "A president can easily explain gut issues like depressions and wars to people, but how do you translate the complex, sophisticated economic issues of the 60's?" Got any idea? Not offhand, was the understated reply of the year. "You'd better talk to Ted Sorensen about it," he prodded, and then later, as I edged out the door, he reminded me again. "Be sure to call Ted about the gold flow." When I dutifully telephoned Ted, an astounded Sorensen wondered why on earth I was suddenly interested in the gold flow? The President, he said, had called him right after my departure with instructions to brief me. I left the White House with several pounds of facts and charts which I haven't penetrated to this day.

After he lost the Vice-Presidential nomination to Estes Kefauver in 1956, JFK became the hottest tourist attraction in Washington. He zoomed to the top of the popularity polls after Adlai Stevenson's defeat, but Washington dopesters, the veteran neutrals as well as the liberal Democrats still in love with Adlai, assured one and all that Kennedy was not to be taken seriously. He was too much the golden boy, they said, too slickly publicized, too dominated by free-spending Daddy, Ambassador Joseph P. Kennedy. His religion and his age were all wrong, they said, and so was his wife. How could chic Jackie, who went to the Senate Rackets Committee hearings with such socialites as Babs Paley and Mrs. Winston Guest, possibly appeal to voters who preferred middle-aged neutrality in candidates' wives?

Senator Kennedy was infinitely better than the superficial glamour image which dogged and irked him. To a writer who profiled him for the book, "Candidates 1960," he mildly protested that the piece had an "overriding flavor of *jeunesse dorée*," too much gilded youth, too little spelling out of his serious views on the Presidency. Another writer about this time trailed Kennedy to a reception at the Spanish Embassy. It plainly bored the Senator after a few minutes. "These do's are a big waste of time," he muttered. "Nobody talks about anything. At least, at this one, the Greek Ambassador came up with a serious discussion of their refugee problem." In Columbia, South Carolina, where he'd gone to pick up another honorary degree, the smooth political image seemed nowhere apparent when he spoke out at a press conference with startling candor in support of the Supreme Court decision on school desegregation. It was the law of the land, and he stood by it, he said. He knew this could not endear him to the same southern delegations that had supported him for Vice President. After his Pulitzer Prize book, *Profiles in Courage,* Kennedy was twitted by Senator Lyndon Johnson as a man who had more profile than courage, but the line was more clever than apt. Kennedy was canny, he could be devious in maneuvers, but he had plenty of courage with his convictions. Perhaps a more accurate criticism of Kennedy in the pre-Presidential days was that while he had the courage of his convictions, he wasn't overburdened with convictions.

After the South Carolina statement, a conservative Southern publisher voiced a number of uncomplimentary views about liberals, Negroes, and Catholics. He was asked why, in light of these sentiments, he was supporting Kennedy for President. Well, he replied, Kennedy had a splendid war record, and besides "old Joe would keep him in line." That was another myth without foundation. Kennedy once said privately of his father that "he and I disagree on almost everything." After one violent dinner table argument with his father, Jack left the table rather than continue.

The father-and-son relationship was intimate, intertwined and sometimes abrasive. Ambassador Kennedy once complained heatedly (an adjective that fits most of his activities) to Harper & Bros., publisher of his son's bestseller *Profiles in Courage,* that the publishing house was not promoting the book as energetically as it might. Evan Thomas of Harper's took the brunt of the elder Kennedy's fire chiefly because he had edited the book. Thomas was also the son of Norman Thomas, perennial Socialist Party candidate for President. One evening Evan Thomas and Jack Kennedy had a drink at 21 in New York and discussed the situation. Thomas asked if Senator Kennedy couldn't do something to moderate the intensity of his father's objections. The conversation went like this:

Kennedy: "Look, you have a famous and controversial father. Do you agree with him on everything?"

Thomas: "No."

Kennedy: "Does he dictate what you do?"

Thomas: "No."

Kennedy: "But you love him, don't you?"

Thomas: "Yes, I do."

Kennedy: "Well, so do I. Let's not get upset. My father thinks he's helping me."

Kennedy accepted his father's financial assistance, listened to his wily dissection of men and methods, let his father operate in his name in lining up party bosses and, more important, in putting pressure on party bosses. But when it came to policy, they were usually wide apart. He was more amused than annoyed by his father's wrathful threats to destroy foes of his son. He laughed at Joe's high-octane tactics, particularly in areas in which the destiny of the nation really didn't ride on the outcome.

Son knew that the father would move the world for him if he could— even though they disagreed on the need for the moving and even on the nature of the world itself. If the father-domination theme was a myth, Kennedy's heralded desire for privacy definitely was not. He was a respecter of privacy. He granted it for others and he demanded it for himself. One lady magazine writer never got a second interview with the Senator for reasons even she probably doesn't know. She had arrived on the Senator's doorstep, fresh from profiling a movie star, and she thought she'd titillate JFK with some delicious unprintable gossip about the actor. "Her idea of establishing rapport," said Kennedy with distaste, "was to tell me the actor was a bed wetter. That didn't inspire confidence."

For all the generalized glamour portraits of him, whose publicity value he knew full well, Kennedy increasingly shied from any attempt to depict the intimate Kennedy household. "What do you want to talk to Jackie for?" he asked one writer. What he thought was more important was his own view on the new minimum wage bill then in the Senate hopper. Jackie emulated her husband in avoiding the intimate lens. To one interviewer, she said: "Oh, please don't ask me about Jack's complexes like all the others. All they ask me is: Doesn't Jack have a complex about his father, and isn't Bobby driven by complexes about Jack? How silly and how dreary!"

In time people came to agree with Sorensen that his candidate was impressive; a bona fide intellectual without the onus of egghead— and with an unusual penchant for action. Still, few could take seriously Ted's cocksure confidence that here was the next President of the United States. There were many doubts during the campaign. Typical of liberals and intellectuals who felt uneasy about JFK, the candidate, was Eric Sevareid who fretted: "In his heart every Republican I know is a little uneasy about Nixon, every other Democrat is uneasy about Kennedy. Not because of his youth, toughness, church, or father's quick money . . . the managerial revolution has come to politics—Nixon & Kennedy is its first completely packaged product . . . junior executives trained in the home office with unerring eye on the big chance."

Then, suddenly, after all the doubts and the emotional turmoil of an American political campaign, here he was the President-elect by a margin as thin as the lock he had clipped from his forehead to make him appear more mature. He was in Palm Beach, the inauguration only a few weeks off, and he had many things to do pronto—complete his new administration, staff the White House, fill seventy-five key cabinet and policy posts.

I came to Palm Beach on a mission of lesser importance, to profile the new First Lady and to embroider the text for a picture layout on the new First Family. John, Jr., was only a few weeks out of the incubator and Mrs. Kennedy, still recuperating from his Cesarean birth, was seeing no reporters, although she had consented to answer a written questionnaire. The questions were less than provocative, but she answered them. What had struck her about JFK on first meeting? He was amusing, intelligent, she replied. What had her father been like? "Same sense of humor as my husband." How did her husband relax? "He never does."

Since the primary source was unavailable, who should one talk to about Mrs. Kennedy? "The President," said Salinger promptly. No matter how irrelevant or unstatesmanlike a writer's errand during the next three years, it was to be ever thus. The person who was most seeable was Himself.

Armed with pencil and notebook, I rang the doorbell at the sprawling, stucco Kennedy mansion by the sea after passing the cordon of Secret Service men.

The implements of a reporter's trade confused the person who answered the door, Ambassador Joseph Kennedy. "Oh, so you're the new secretary?" he asked brightly. No, I was there to interview the President. "Well, come right in," invited the President's father. Still, one had to hesitate at the door of the living room, for there, his back to me, was the President-elect in swimming trunks, bivouacked in a deep couch, his feet propped on a coffee table. He never in those days seemed to sit in a chair. He curled up in one like a corkscrew or sat with a leg dangling over an arm. He was on the phone now, talking about appointments and plans for the Inauguration. While I still hesitated, the Ambassador gave me a little shove: "Go right on in."

His phoning over, a very tanned, high-spirited JFK called out breezily: "Hi, Laurer." Would I like a look at John? And there was the baby, napping in the sun in a buggy. All that could be seen of him was his bare bottom. Of course, one had to murmur that he sure looked like a fine baby. Had I brought a swim suit? asked JFK. No? How silly, when we could have gone swimming. Anyway, come along and he'd show me some paintings his wife had done. They turned out to be bright water colors, done in sophisticated yet childlike style, à la Ludwig Bemelmans, with themes that were predominantly inside family jokes. They revealed much about her, more perhaps than her nonchalantly chic attire, or the wide-eyed naiveté of her public appearances. In one gay, mad scene, painted for Joe Kennedy's private collection, she had what appeared to be zillions of Kennedys romping about on a beach. Overhead trailed a banner: "You can't take it with you. Dad's got it all." On an opposite wall hung a Jackie original in which pickets marched with signs: "Put Jackie and Joan (Ted Kennedy's wife) back in American clothes," a spoof of the campaign rhubarb over their allegedly all-Parisian wardrobes.

Spying a new framed photograph of her, the President had an idea: Wouldn't that make a smashing cover for a magazine? It was the kind of picture of her that he liked. She was casual, windblown, sunburned, in a simple checked gingham dress.

Out by the pool Ted Sorensen sat at a typewriter, pecking away at a new draft of the inaugural speech: "Ask not what your country can do for you, but what you can do for your country." As we sat in beach chairs, the background sound of the talk was the steady, rat-a-tat of that typewriter. The Kennedy ambiance was ever the same: electrically charged informality. Mrs. Lincoln scurried up with letters to sign, and in her friendly, folksy way said: "Why how nice to see you," as though the meeting had made her day.

JFK asked if I were coming to the inaugural festivities. No? Why not? Hadn't been invited, I replied. Well, okay, he forthwith invited me. Then, in a tone of voice which clearly said, "Let's get this over with for

God's sake," he asked what I wanted to know about Jackie. He ticked off qualities he found remarkable in his wife, including her excellent memory and her gifts as a linguist. Kennedy advised a talk with his brother Ted about Jackie, for she had helped Ted out with a college theme. As a matter of fact, he said, Jackie had suggested the theme, a comparison between Goya's paintings and a new Spanish novel called "The Hive."

In this poolside talk about the President-elect's wife, the name of Dorothy Kilgallen, *New York Journal-American* columnist and TV panelist, was mentioned. Miss Kilgallen, during the campaign, had written some waspish items about the Kennedys.

"If you want to make an interesting bet," she had written that September, "wager that Mrs. Jack Kennedy won't have a baby 'around election day' in November, as advertised. The chic, beautiful, intelligent, appealing Mrs. Kennedy is being kept under wraps because the Democratic party bosses think her looks are too far out for the 'moms' in the Midwest to digest. They die every time she makes an appearance looking like a fashion magazine model—so they'd rather she didn't appear."

Had Kennedy heard of this particular Kilgallen item? "Sure," he replied, "but what can you expect from a dame who's in love with . . . ," an entertainer of whom JFK apparently did not have a high opinion. Once again, out of the blue, protruded Kennedy's antenna for gossip. How did a President-elect learn of this inside, inside rumor that had been confined largely to the smoky rooms of P. J. Clarke's, the columnist's hangout on Third Avenue in Manhattan?

He had a sudden impish thought. Why was I pursuing a profile on Jackie? "Hell, you don't even know her. Why don't you do a piece about me?" Well, I hedged, maybe he'd been "over-exposed." Where was the fresh material? Hang around, he said, there'd be some.

Abruptly, he cut off the chat about Jackie. He switched to Fidel Castro, the man who was to plague him for years. What, he wondered, was Castro's messianic appeal. Could it be compared to Hitler's in the 1930's? If not, why not? Why, he asked, those long, haranguing speeches? These speeches obviously baffled JFK, whose own oratory was terse and non-inflammatory. The long Castro rallies intrigued Kennedy—or was he putting me on? Did Fidel, he wondered, have any personal life at all? A love life? Kennedy had had a taste of mob adulation during the campaign, particularly in the final, frenzied days, but he talked about it clinically, detached, as though it mystified and amused rather than elated him. He seemed genuinely puzzled about the mystique of a Latin *caudillo*. Kennedy was the complete contrast to Castro; cool, self-possessed, a disciplined rationalist. The emotional appeal of a Castro seemed to elude him; and along with some people I then wondered whether Kennedy for all his brightness had a visceral understanding of the angry revolutionists loose in the world.

●

At the outset, columnist Walter Lippmann comparing him with assorted Chief Executives found him a more "serious man than FDR, more physically akin to robust Teddy, and more politically educated and disciplined than either." But he, too, raised the big doubt: would the Boston thoroughbred have FDR's vital gift—"knowing how the masses felt?" That cool, dry, downbeat approach, his third person detachment about himself and his fortunes, was likened to the stance of junior officers in World War II; there was little of the evangelist about him. It might be the manner of his generation but it did not seem the stuff of which national heroes are made. When asked early what he hoped to be labeled as President, he replied "I hope to be responsible." What had been his reaction to FDR's death? "I had no deeply traumatic experience." James Reston of *The New York Times* once in a private talk asked him what he wanted to achieve by the time he left 1600 Pennsylvania Avenue—did he feel the need of some goal to guide his day-to-day decisions and priorities? There was a "ghastly pause" until the talk turned to tangible problems, and then he reeled off a torrent of statistics about the difficulties of organizing nations at different levels of economic development.

Comparing him to another born-to-wealth candidate, Nelson Rockefeller, the ebullient, folksy New York Governor seemed the more natural, assured glandular politician—visibly blooming when he plunged into a crowd with that big "hi fella" greeting. Yet, close up, the Governor was a wary, nonconfiding, arms-length politician, even with long-time associates. JFK seemed to be the polar opposite—at his best in face to face encounter, but uneasy in a pushing, grasping, adoring crowd. One editor exposed to JFK at a White House lunch spelled it out: "Everything is handled in such an informal manner that you feel at ease. The President asked us for our opinion on a number of matters . . . he speaks so frankly about things that you get a feeling that he trusts you and that he is taking you into his confidence."

Although he was visibly impatient with stuffy people, places, "bleeders," bores, "people with nothing upstairs," and though his world, as one observer noted, seemed bounded by Harvard Yard and Palm Beach, he was in his own curious way at home with a stunning variety of humans—politicians and journalists (above all professional breeds); the products of Boston fourth-floor walk-up flats; the jet set. New leaders of Black Africa, as one Ambassador said, thought of him as a personal friend because "he talked the language of the young leaders of this new, turbulent world, because in their mid-forties he was one of them . . . he knew their problems and made them understand ours. It was because of President Kennedy, because they had talked to him and knew what he was trying to do, that the leaders of Black Africa have been so understanding of the torment and the violence of our own struggle for freedom and equality here at home."

He inspired gung-ho idolatry in his staff, but some young liberal Democratic senators who should have been his natural allies by 1963 were grumbling away about their "lack of communication" with New Frontiersmen. One senatorial assistant complained: "I don't dig that tight-lipped terse approach of those guys in the White House. I want to talk issues, they like to play hard-boiled operator. They've even got the professors doing it."

But Big Policy aside, there was no denying he created a bracing climate in Washington, in which it was possible to be critical, argumentative with a President—and he was never a dull man to watch. Once, having been closeted with a particular head of government for two days, JFK went into the Rose Garden for one of those ceremonies Presidents have to endure. A reporter, puzzled by a particularly opaque JFK sentence during his brief address to a religious group, asked Salinger to find out exactly what he meant. "The President said to tell you he doesn't know what he meant," came back the reply. "He said that is just the way he gets after two days with so-and-so."

On that first splendid state trip to France, a lady reporter smuggled herself into an anteroom at the Paris Ballet during the intermission, where Presidents Charles De Gaulle and JFK were sipping champagne and talking to the dancers. That sneaky maneuver delighted Kennedy who introduced her to his eminence De Gaulle as a "friend from Washington." Photographers were let in for a quick historical portrait, then dismissed with an imperious flick of the De Gaulle finger. *Entre nous,* said the lady party crasher to JFK, "Don't you wish that you could control photographers like that?" "You must remember," he responded, "that I wasn't recalled to office as my country's savior."

At White House dinners, he'd wing off similarly unsettling remarks to stir up a sluggish conversation: once he doubted that Pope John was all he was cracked up to be in the press. "You Protestants are building him up," he suggested. Even the Anglican Church headed by Queen Elizabeth got a spoofing: "How can you believe in a church headed by a girl like that?"

On a last November weekend in 1963, he and his wife and old friends Mr. and Mrs. Benjamin Bradlee went to his newly built retreat near Atoka, Virginia. Mrs. K handed the President a few lumps of sugar to feed the resident Irish pony, Leprechaun. The sugar ran out fast, but

Leprechaun in pursuit of more goodies seemed on the verge of nibbling at the President himself. To visiting White House photographer Cecil Stroughton who often took informal snaps for the family album, JFK cracked: "Keep shooting Captain. You're about to watch a President being eaten by a horse."

Hyannis was his cup of tea, but oh-so-social Newport, Rhode Island, wasn't. Summers, as a dutiful husband, he'd spend days or weeks in the stronghold of old-line Eastern society where his wife's mother, Mrs. Hugh Auchincloss and Jackie's stepfather dwelled in splendor on magnificent Hammersmith Farm. Novelist William Styron and his wife, who'd been guests at a White House cultural bash, and sailed with the Kennedys at the Cape, found themselves in Newport during a Presidential visit. They were out sailing, when a Coast Guard cutter knifed close to their boat with an invite from the Kennedys to drop by, casual as that. Remembering the old-shoe informality of Hyannis, they went straightaway to the party without changing from dungarees to find themselves the Odd Couple at a dressed-to-the-nines gathering. As they hovered uneasily on the party fringes, JFK strolled over and asked: "How did they manage to get *you* here? They had enough trouble getting *me* here."

As a Senator, vacationing in a posh Jamaica resort, a maverick JFK showed up for a party at which formal attire was obligatory—he conformed, but only halfway. He wore dinner jacket and bow tie—with shorts. During this interlude in Round Hill, his Senate office had issued a JFK statement calling for help for the unemployed. This prompted an ironic remark from Senator Kenneth Keating of New York about sponsors of the poor who whiled away time in high price Caribbean resorts. During his speech, Keating was slipped a sketch from Kennedy, of a noose dangling from a gallows, inscribed: "From the gang at Round Hill."

Some things bored him utterly. Enveigled by his wife into attending a Washington horse show, he was heard muttering "Let me out of here." "We didn't take him to symphony concerts because we couldn't keep him awake," said his friend William Walton. "He liked action movies. It's no secret he loved 'Spartacus' (a wide-screen spectacular)." But the night Jackie had a new *avant garde* "in" French movie "Jules and Jim" screened at the White House, he up and walked out. Even baseball, he once complained, was a bit slow for him.

Yet when someone, or something piqued his interest—or sympathies —he could be the despair of appointment secretary Kenneth O'Donnell whose job, it was said, was not to keep visitors out of the Presidential office, but the restless President *in*.

A fifteen-minute ceremony might stretch to thirty or forty-five minutes, raising havoc with the official schedule. In the spring of 1963, four blind

students were ushered into the Presidential presence, flanked by their parents, to get accolades for scholastic achievement. Awards duly handed out, he looked around and asked "Where's the guy from Harvard?" That was Patrick Peppe, who was shortly graduating as a history major in the top 5 per cent of his Harvard class. "Where's your father?" he asked young Patrick, after some old-school-tie palaver. Father Peppe was a one-armed Italian immigrant who ran a newsstand in the New York Bronx. Just where was Mr. Peppe's newsstand? On the Grand Concourse Boulevard? He'd lived in The Bronx as a boy himself, said JFK, and could wager he'd bought papers from that very stand. The Peppes must have their visit memorialized in a White House photograph. How about the relatives, wouldn't they like copies? And what about the people back home? Back home? In the old home town in Italy—surely they'd want to see how far Patrick Peppe, son of an immigrant, had come.

Another thought: Patrick, the history major, and his three fellow awards winners, might be interested in the Presidential desk, an historical piece of furniture Mrs. Kennedy had unearthed in a dark corner of the White House. Queen Victoria had given it to President Rutherford Hayes; and it was fashioned of timbers from an old ship, the H.M.S. *Resolute*. Just run your fingers over it, he urged his guests. They could feel for themselves how handsomely it was carved. Now on their White House tour there were other historical objects they mustn't miss, he'd brief the guide himself about just which ones.

These Rose Garden ceremonials, greetings to foreign dignitaries, pep talks for student groups, endorsements of charities, all required some brief Presidential utterance. Staffers would come up with brief remarks tailored for the occasion. Gettysburg addresses were scarcely required since the newspapers gave these tribal rites only a few lines mention. But this word-man seldom left a script intact, scribbling in changes at the last minute, honing a phrase, cutting out an inept adjective. His secretary, Mrs. Lincoln, recalls the day he greeted the first group of foreign students. (In their overpowering enthusiasm, they almost trampled JFK underfoot when he stepped into the garden to say more personal hellos after the official greeting). He glanced at the prepared speech for the first time as he walked from his office to the Portico steps, and then with not another glance gave it almost verbatim, sharpening the text as he spoke and throwing in his own ad libs.

Arthur Schlesinger, Jr., ghosted his first annual TV appeal for the United Fund campaign. Kennedy speed-read the words, turned toward the three network cameras—and delivered his own fresh pitch without a pause, using not a phrase from the pre-written material.

Once someone theorized that he had inherited his IBM memory, the ability to soak up facts, figures, ideas, and odd pieces of information with extraordinary speed from his canny Irish father, and that his charm came from his mother Rose Kennedy. All wrong, JFK told his sister Eunice Shriver. It was the other way round. If he had "charm," it came from Ambassador Joe Kennedy; any "brains" came from his mother. During his father's absences it was Rose Kennedy who would turn the family dinner table into quick quiz sessions. "What's today," she'd ask her brood. "July 14th," they'd chorus. No, no, she chided, it was a national holiday, but which one? Any Kennedy was expected to know the answer, "Bastille Day."

In his own quick-quizzing, he often seemed to "compartmentalize" people by subjects. If he knew your area of interest was Latin America, he'd harp on that subject. ("Why don't you get interested in Africa," he once asked me, apparently feeling my horizons needed expanding). Chatting with a journalist who'd just written a best-selling political novel, he ragged him about its theme and its sales. From another, who'd been trailing campaigning Governor Rockefeller, he wanted to know all about "Rocky's" style of operating, sizing up that potential antagonist. Skimming an architectural magazine, JFK spotted a design drawing of the U.S. Pavilion for the New York World's Fair. The original, said Bill Walton, his unofficial architecture advisor, looked like a "giant plant stand," and he got instant phone orders from a riled President: "Do something." The architect quickly sketched a new design which "wasn't great," according to Walton, but it wasn't an "embarrassment."

Thirty seconds after Kennedy met the University of Minnesota's Walter Heller in the 1960 campaign, he was peppering the economist with questions on his specialty. "Do you think we can really make the 5 per cent national growth rate?" he asked, as he changed clothes in a Minneapolis hotel. Typically, he was running an hour behind his campaign schedule, but still he fired queries at Heller for six, seven minutes. Sample "How come the German economy prospered so well at 5 per cent interest rates and yet you fellows want easy money?" Heller, later chairman of Kennedy's Council of Economic Advisers, recalls that the President read through every one of some 400 to 500 technical memoranda, some ten pages long, sent to him on specific issues.

Judgments about Kennedy were subject to change swiftly. Generally, men began by underestimating his ability and wound up by respecting it. A few, of course, went the other route, but with the intellectual community, particularly, Kennedy gained in favor over the years.

Arthur Goldberg, when he was Secretary of Labor, watched Kennedy in the early House years and later recorded his impressions: "When he was a Congressman and I was a labor lawyer, I spent a lot of time educating him. He was a practical student, not an academic one, and he left to the scholar the pleasure of speculation for its own sake. Many times you found he'd read something, but he never made a point of what he had read . . . I thought he was a young, impressionable Congressman, but about 1956 I began to be impressed by him. If you read the record on the Landrum-Griffin bill, you'll find he was damn good."

John Cogley, then editor of the liberal Catholic weekly, *Commonweal,* recalls how difficult it was to peg JFK permanently. His first impressions of the young Senator were negative. Cogley attended when Kennedy shared the dais with Clare Boothe Luce at a Freedom House dinner in New York. "I thought he was one of the worst speakers I'd ever heard," says Cogley. "He was dull, dry, he mumbled, he didn't say anything. He was, frankly, awful. I couldn't believe this man seriously wanted to be President of the United States." Then two years later on a TV show, Kennedy seemed a "completely different man. I found myself fascinated by the way his mind worked, he passed up one opportunity after another to be a phoney, to hedge on issues—he became frankly my first political hero, but you couldn't convince the big name 'liberal-intellectuals' even after his nomination that he was to be taken seriously. I kept arguing that it was JFK, not Stevenson, for all his gift for language, who was the really bright one, the real intellectual. He was a new breed of political cat who wasn't bashful or hesitant about seeking power—and what was wrong with that?" Typical of the doubters was Robert Maynard Hutchins, who'd been a boy wonder at twenty-nine, as president of the University of Chicago. "What's Kennedy ever done?" he'd ask. "What's he for or against?"

Four years later, Martin Luther King, Jr., civil rights leader, gave an answer. "One of the basic things about him—he had the ability to respond to creative pressure . . . I think that historians will have to record that he vacillated like Lincoln but he lifted the cause far above the political level. He grew until the day of the assassination."

The only trait Kennedy really couldn't abide in people was dullness. He enjoyed the brain-trust intellectuals of the White House, like Sorensen and McGeorge Bundy, whose domain was a world apart from the equally cherished political technicians, Larry O'Brien and Kenny O'Donnell of the Irish Mafia (a nickname they didn't much care for, at first). When Mrs. Kennedy was away, it was Dave Powers with whom JFK had breakfast. Old journalist buddies, such as Charles Bartlett and Ben Bradlee, came by for private dinners. Then there was his set of relaxing friends, such as Under Secretary of the Navy Paul (Red) Fay, who swam, walked, or went to the movies with him. These were chiefly men of his own age, World War II friends he'd known for years and who didn't overtax his mind. His wife and his family were yet another world. He wasn't the kind of husband who

26

wanted to discuss his daily work with Jackie. "He wanted me as a wife," she said. "He seldom brought home his problems, except once in a while the serious ones."

Some were puzzled that this man who communicated such empathy to leaders of Black Africa counted among his closest friends George Smathers of Florida, a senator who supported racial segregation and who seldom backed New Frontier policy, racial or otherwise. Kennedy and Smathers were young buck friends in the House of Representatives. Smathers had been an usher at his wedding. Theirs was an early friendship that surmounted major political differences. Kennedy forever needled his old friend. At a fund-raising dinner at Miami Beach, JFK said, "I actually came down here tonight to pay a debt of obligation to an old friend and faithful advisor. He and I came to the 80th Congress together and have been associated for many years, and I regard him as one of my most valuable counselors in moments of great personal and public difficulty.

"In 1952, when I was thinking about running for the United States Senate, I went to Senator Smathers and said 'George, what do you think?' He said 'Don't do it. Can't win. Bad year' . . . And in 1960 I was wondering whether I ought to run in the West Virginia primary. 'Don't do it. That state you can't possibly carry.' And actually the only time I really got nervous about the whole matter at the Democratic Convention of 1960 was just before the balloting and George came up and he said 'I think it looks pretty good for you.' "

That was the Kennedy needle, with humor. He could jab the needle in without humor, as he did to some 1,000 Ambassadors and lesser diplomats of the Foreign Service. Bluntly, undiplomatically, he made it plain he felt too many of them were living in the past, didn't know their jobs, were inclined to buck-pass decisions to a few overworked men in Washington, and didn't get out of their Embassies enough to meet the natives. "Instead of becoming merely experts in diplomatic history or in current clippings of *The New York Times,*" he scolded, "now you have to involve yourselves in every element of foreign life—labor, the class struggle, cultural affairs, and all the rest—attempting to predict in what direction the forces will move. [You] must know every important facet of life in the United States with particular regard to the great reforms of the thirties, the forties and fifties, so as to represent the United States powerfully and with vigor." British correspondent Alistair Cooke noted that such paragons were in short supply in all the foreign services of the world, but JFK should be given high marks for his great expectations. "Even the enemies of Franklin Roosevelt," said Cooke, "used to say that at least he would be blessed for having planted three million trees. The foes of John F. Kennedy may similarly admit that he managed to get the U.S. represented abroad by men who knew two languages, had some acquaintance with the native culture, and dined with beatniks as easily as bankers."

JFK had always shunned routine. He'd rather drive a car than be driven. As a senator when he was impatient for some new information, he'd often bypass the staff and get it himself, calling an obscure civil servant, an undersecretary, or a reporter.

For all of his celerity of mind, you wondered, how did he manage to juggle everything, much less gobble up every publication, domestic and foreign, worth reading, scan every fiftieth letter of some 30,000 written him weekly . . . and then in a photographic session, take time out to notice approvingly a photographer's new shoes? Once when I saw him, his attention was momentarily riveted by an inexpensive piece of costume jewelry I was wearing. It was a gold cross studded with fake jewels—and for two or three minutes he spun off questions about it: what kind of cross was it, Maltese perhaps? Was it real? No? It looked it. Was it U.S. or European made? An Italian import? That triggered some thoughts about Italian crafts-manship, how they produced such baubles so well and at such low cost.

Ted Sorensen, who styled himself a "generalist," meaning his duties ranged from speech-writing to advising on Berlin, had one plausible explanation for this particular Kennedy operating style. The Boss, he said, had a remarkably "compartmentalized" mind. "I can see him a half dozen times a day—on matters like Berlin, aid to parochial schools, the upcoming budget. He seldom, if ever, refers to a previous conversation. Once a subject is discussed, it's dropped."

Ernest L. Barcella, UPI Washington Bureau Manager, once kept a log of roughly five minutes of Presidential activity during a noon hour. It went like this:

12:52 P.M. JFK bounces from his Oval Office into the adjoining office of Mrs. Lincoln. He read, signed letters, and tossed off instructions as he went along.

"Congratulate him for this," he ordered. It was the appointment of a North Carolina judge. "Give this to Ted Reardon," he said. It was a letter from the head of a New York advertising firm. He autographed a PT-boat picture of himself and ordered: "That's for the museum in Tennessee."

A White House photographer was at his elbow. Asked JFK of the PT-boat shot: "Say, is this the only thing we've got?"

"Do you want it touched up?" asked the photographer.

"Yes," said the President, "take the white stuff out."

Then back to Mrs. Lincoln and a letter from a member of the White House police combat team which had set a new record score in a pistol-shooting match. "Good," he said. "Why don't you congratulate them?"

He put aside another letter. "I want to read this," he said.

Then an afterthought: "I asked somebody this morning to write a letter to Prince Bernhard."

In less than five minutes, he had read and signed seven letters, read five more and autographed two pictures. A few minutes later, downstairs for his daily swim, he called from the White House pool to ask about the guest list for the Pakistan dinner. He wanted to go over the names again.

Kennedy was always looking, listening, reaching, reading, and he expected the same intensity in other officials. This quest for knowledge was no late development. Unorthodox Chicago financier J. Patrick Lannan recalls running into the young Kennedy in 1945 in White Castle Springs, Arizona, where Jack Kennedy was trying to recuperate from the malaria he'd contracted in the South Pacific during the War. Lannan advised him that any man going into politics needed to study the labor movement and its politics. JFK immediately asked his father's office in New York to accumulate and air mail to him the best written sources on organized labor. When the 3-foot box arrived, recalls Lannan, Kennedy "lined the books up in a row on the table and read straight through from left to right."

A year after the meeting in Arizona, Lannan met Kennedy again in London where JFK, then a newsman, was covering a Winston Churchill campaign. The Kennedy hotel suite invariably was jammed, each afternoon, with an "impressive group of young English veterans. They were the bright ones just mustered out, not the sick, third-generation crowd, but the real ones, and they'd talk until three in the morning about the world that was to come." One was David Ormsby Gore, the attractive young Englishman who was to become Ambassador to the U.S. during New Frontier days and forge links between his country and the new President. "He was a pro," remembers Lannan of JFK. "I've never known a human being that I've come to connect with greater competence. He was like when the Yankees play baseball. This is a great country. Its vitality and strength needed to be prodded. He knew how."

The ability, JFK once said, "to do things well, and to do them with precision and with modesty, attracts us all." This prismatic man was above all things competent—and he was also a man who never missed a trick. He wrote his best-selling *Profiles in Courage* flat on his back, recuperating from a spinal operation that was near fatal. Then shortly before its publication, noting that the Pulitzer Prize entries in the biography category were a bit thin for 1954, called his publisher and urged the publication date be moved up to qualify. The date could not be moved, but he still walked off with the Pulitzer in 1955.

Yet this "pragmatic" Kennedy had a predilection for literature and poetry whose themes were lost causes and the poignancy of men dying

young. His wife said he loved Irish poetry "not the sentimental verse people often think of as Irish but the poetry of their struggle for freedom, full of bitterness and despair." "My husband was a romantic," she wrote in the summer of 1964, "although he didn't like people to know that."

Back in 1952, when he was running for the Senate against Republican Henry Cabot Lodge, not a single important Massachusetts paper was for him until the *Boston Post*, now defunct, suddenly switched from Lodge to Kennedy. In 1958 Senate hearings, John Fox, owner of the *Post*, revealed that after that endorsement, Ambassador Joe Kennedy lent the ailing paper $500,000. Funny coincidence, thought a digging reporter, and went round to ask the Senator about it. It would only be fair, said Kennedy, to get his father's version of the incident, to clear up any implication that the Kennedys had "bought" the paper to get the endorsement. From the Joseph Kennedy office came the explanation: "The loan as mentioned was made after the election as a purely commercial transaction—for sixty days with full collateral, at full interest, and was fully repaid in time, and was simply one of many commercial transactions in which this office has participated."

That information in hand, the reporter was departing, when Kennedy couldn't resist leveling, with a grin: "We didn't have a single major paper in Massachusetts. Hell, we had to buy that paper."

That candor, publicly, helped him win the election, for "electing the first Catholic President was like running the four-minute mile or orbiting the earth in space," as writer William Shannon assessed the feat in his book *The American Irish*.

Some of his staffers were appalled by the ground rules hammered out for the fateful Houston Texas Ministerial Association confrontation by advisers James Wine, a staff member of the National Council of Churches, and Catholic liberal John Cogley. It was to be a no-holds-barred session. "No Presidential candidate should submit himself to that kind of questioning," grumbled a Kennedy man. "At least the questions should be written out."

(Just before the Houston Meeting, he was scheduled to appear in San Antonio at the Alamo, shrine of Texas independence—on which occasion he also intended to grapple with the Catholic issue. Cogley in Washington got an eleventh-hour call from a Kennedy adviser, saying the candidate was honing his speech, and could he dig up some figures on how many American Catholics had died at the Alamo? Frantic research through capital bookstores yielded nary a clue, apart from a casualty list heavily studded with Irish-American names. JFK finessed that beautifully with the line: "For there was no religious test at the Alamo . . . side by side with Bowie and Crockett died McCafferty and Bailey and Carey, but no one knows whether they were Catholic or not.")

Kennedy himself was a bit startled by the arrangements for the Houston meeting, and confessed he was nervous about the upcoming confrontation; also he was losing his voice. Aboard the family plane, the *Caroline*, he asked Cogley to field him some tough questions he might be asked. Sample: would he object to going to a Protestant funeral service if a Supreme Court Justice died? For some two hours, JFK scribbled answers on a note pad and at one juncture wrote: "It is hard for a Harvard man to answer questions in theology. I imagine my answers tonight will cause heartburn in Fordham and Boston College." The grilling went on for another half hour, then he cut it off. "That's all. I either make it or I don't."

That critical night, he had to cope with another problem—diplomatic. Texans LBJ and House Speaker Sam Rayburn were part of the entourage, and assumed they'd be sharing the Houston platform with him. Privately, JFK was deadset against it. He saw, theorizes Cogley, "the drama inherent in a Boston Catholic Irishman alone facing the Texas Protestants," without the supporting prop of VIP Texans. His solution—he had two speaking engagements scheduled in Houston that night. The "major" speech he urged Johnson to take care of, though it wouldn't permit time for Johnson to attend the ministerial meeting.

"I believe," JFK said that night, "in an America where the separation of church and state is absolute—where no Catholic prelate would tell the President (should he be a Catholic), how to act, and no Protestant minister would tell his parishioners for whom to vote. I am not the Catholic candidate for President; I am the Democratic party's candidate for President who also happens to be a Catholic. I do not speak for my church on public matters and the church does not speak for me." His performance that night in Houston all but took the religious issue right out of the campaign.

No one, it seemed, ever really spoke for John Kennedy, not Sorensen, nor Schlesinger, nor Salinger, nor even Bobby. He spoke for himself with the lightning shifts of tongue and mood that could go from Tennyson to economic growth rates, from Indonesia to California politics, from an appeal to humanity to a mordant little inside joke about life in the White House.

He never stood still long enough to let one make a final, definitive assessment of him. In the last year, he changed; he had grown visibly in office and he had aged. After the death of his infant son Patrick in the early fall of 1963, he had moods of pensive sadness and he and Mrs. Kennedy dined increasingly alone without guests. I sensed this new shadow on his ebullience the last time I saw him in October, only a few weeks before the Dallas trip. Now the White House had come to seem his natural habitat. But there was a sadness about him, a somber, sobering quality that I had never glimpsed before.

Had he lived, some said he would have become a great President in a second term. History can only guess now. His time was a brief one, like a sudden, last surge of sunlight at dusk. But in that brief time, he brought courage, rationality, spaciousness, and the fresh wind of youth to American life.

With John F. Kennedy, a new outlook, a new generation had taken over and many Americans shakily realized it was their own.

1961: Only a few months in office, the new President had just delivered a foreign VIP to Blair House. Then on the ride home to the White House he brushed back a wisp of her hair. This is one of her favorite pictures of them both.

Griffith Stadium, 1962. JFK threw a fast curve (having practiced his pitching in the Rose Garden) on opening day to the amusement of (left to right) aide Lawrence F. O'Brien; then Secretary of Labor Arthur Goldberg; Senate Majority Leader Mike Mansfield; and old friend Torbert MacDonald, his Harvard roommate, and GOP. Senator Everett Dirksen.

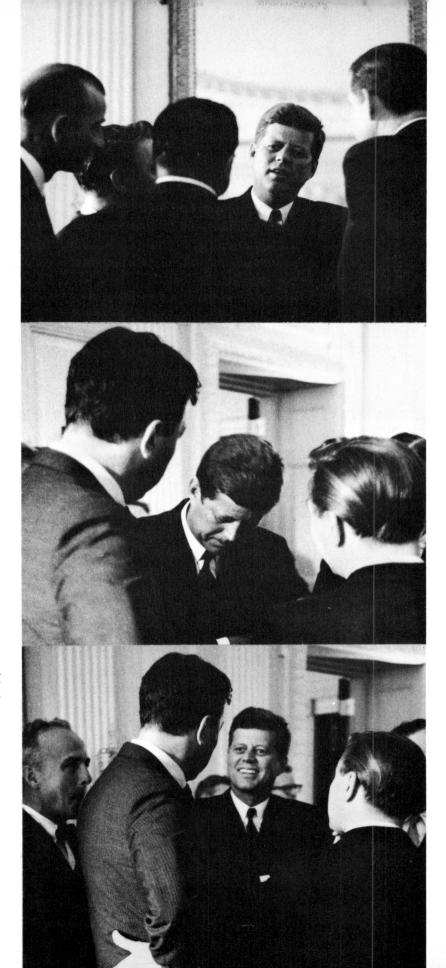

"We just have to exploit his charm and social grace," said Larry O'Brien, arranger of JFK coffee hours with Congressmen in the White House. This one took place in the State Dining Room, 1961, and on hand as usual was the Vice President, Lyndon Johnson.

In less than five minutes of a noon hour, JFK was logged
at having read and signed seven letters, scanned five more,
and autographed two pictures. A glimpse of the working
President with his secretary, Mrs. Lincoln, and McGeorge
Bundy, Special Assistant for National Security Affairs.

JFK strolled out to the South Lawn to see the family off for a Middleburg weekend.

Later that day he joined them.

For 13 days in October, 1962, the Kennedy inner circle sweated out the Cuban missile crisis. On a Sunday, Khrushchev sent word he was pulling the missiles out of Cuba. On Monday, a more relaxed JFK met on the White House portico with Crisis Club members McGeorge Bundy, Paul Nitze, General Maxwell Taylor and Robert McNamara.

*Above: In Vienna, 1961, after coldbath encounters
with Nikita Khrushchev, JFK chatted amiably at
a gala with the Soviet Union's first lady, Nina,
while his mother Rose Kennedy looked on.*

*Left: In Paris, 1961, Charles De Gaulle welcomed JFK with
appropriate grandeur. But most memorable quip of
that trip was made by the U.S. President: "I am the
man who accompanied Jacqueline Kennedy to Paris . . ."*

JFK seemed especially taut on his midwest political tour in October, 1962. What

the listening crowds couldn't know: the Cuban missile crisis was brewing.

"*He was a new breed of political cat who wasn't bashful or hesitant about seeking power—and what was wrong with that?*" Springfield, Illinois, October, 1962.

Two "cool cats." The President and his brother-in-law, Stephen
E. Smith, who probably would have managed JFK's 1964
re-election campaign, met at the Hotel Carlyle in New York City in the
summer of 1963, for a talk about the tangled local political situation.

Blarneying of pompous politicians bored JFK, but he had an elastic schedule when it came to talking to people who interested him. Here, meeting with Peace Corps volunteers in the Rose Garden, he scarcely seems much older than they do.

Nuns
and silly hats

All the cornball accoutrements that go with getting elected to high office in America were alien to the nature of that restrained, detached Harvard man, John F. Kennedy. He did not like to paw or be pawed. He had no yen to "press the flesh," in the overpowering physical manner of President Lyndon Johnson, or ride joyfully in a motorcade arms flung wide open, à la Ike. He recoiled at silly pictures—above all snaps of him in "silly hats," whether they were cowboy, American Legion, Mexican sombrero, or Indian headdresses, and was a wizard at ducking photographers who tried to get same. His disdain was perceptible for the phoney pose, the squashing of the person at huge rallies, the rococo oratory, the hoarse accolades of fellow campaigners.

The millions of females who screamed and bounced and jiggled deliriously at the very sight of JFK passing by couldn't know it, but their frenzied mob adulation left him more bemused than elated. In California, on a campaign train, Governor Pat Brown got quite carried away by the female hysteria Kennedy provoked and yelled: "They're trying to touch him! They're trying to touch him!" "Oh knock it off, Pat," said Kennedy unimpressed.

He might have been more at home on the stump in Great Britain where candidates for the House of Commons campaign in small districts and hone their brains in impromptu give-and-take with hecklers. He was all confidence in the four great national television debates with Richard Nixon. Though toward the end of the jet-maniacal 44,000-mile campaign trail he seemed to be enjoying himself more, the roar of the crowd, the grabbers, the jumpers, and the squeezers, left him not visibly moved.

Columnist Joseph Alsop once brushed the essence of the matter in an argument with James Rowe, a Washington lawyer and former White House assistant. Before the 1960 Democratic convention, Rowe was first a Johnson man and then a pre-convention campaign aide for Senator Hubert Humphrey who also yearned passionately for the White House. Alsop was pro-Kennedy. One day the two men were discussing the pros and cons of their candidates. The exchange heated up and finally Alsop in his most impeccable British-cum-patrician accent shouted at Rowe: "Jim, you'll never understand Jack Kennedy. He's an aristocrat!" Just how Rowe reacted to the implication that *he* was not one has not been recorded.

But Alsop only flicked the essence of Kennedy. JFK was an aristocrat of the mind, not the spirit. There wasn't a sliver of the snob in his make up. He was classy, he was a gentleman, and though gentlemen may curse like longshoremen in private, they contain themselves in public. They do not emote or hang their personal feelings on the line like Monday's wash. He handled opponents, for the most part, with the rapier rather than a bludgeon: when he chose to battle it out in the Wisconsin primary, he said of Senator Symington who declined that test, that the Senator doubtless hoped that Wisconsin would be a "good clean fight with no survivors."

Some candidates have strong glandular responses to the rallies, the maniacal cavalcades and roars of the campaign multitudes—Harold Stassen, perennial wooer of office, was such a man. "Stassen actually quivers at the sight of a campaign plane taking off," observed Edward T. Folliard of the Washington *Post*. A campaign mob unleashes something basic in Lyndon Johnson—he is drawn, as though by a magnet, to the very heart of the shoving, sweating, shouting throngs, eager to palm hands and be one of them.

Now Kennedy had campaigned millions of miles in six election fights for the House, the Senate, and the White House, he had won all the contested primaries, ricocheted through every state, outfoxed all the pros who said he didn't have a chance—but though he'd been seeking the Big Prize since early 1957, campaigning clearly wasn't his favorite sport. His perpetual tardiness on the trail may have been a clue. Once in Philadelphia in the 1960 Presidential trek, he lagged so far behind schedule that he provoked purple oaths in the huge key Philadelphia organization. He was three hours late in all appearances in the city and finally had to cancel some, to the anguish of ward bosses, who had marshalled thousands of flag-waving school kids and party regulars along the route.

The excuse usually ran that Kennedy was being detained by unexpected well-wishers, but perhaps there was something psychological in the habitual way he postponed the moment of truth, the campaign appearance. He would chat five minutes with this person here, ten with that person there, completely absorbed in the discussion. He brushed off aides who pointed at watches and nervously joggled his elbow.

Yet in the strange alchemy of candidate-and-crowd the more reserved and restrained JFK was, the more they screamed their affection. Lawrence O'Brien sensed the paradox and its portent when he first heard the lanky young Kennedy speak in Massachusetts in the late 1940's. "He was an Irish politician with class," he recalled. "You felt that if he got the breaks, he could go all the way, he could be President some day." (Yet toward the windup of that gay Presidential campaign, reporter Murray Kempton recalls an observer saying: "He's starting to go real Mick. He still waves at the crowds and smiles at the girls, but you watch when we pass men working in overalls and he balls up his fist and throws an uppercut. That's Mick. It says 'You keep those rivets coming and I'll do the job.'")

The people, O'Brien sensed, would love that class. The American male may marry the girl next door, but he doesn't want the guy next door as his President. Kennedy, even as Woodrow Wilson and FDR before him, proved that Americans voting for a President respond to the man of breeding, poise, education, and grace.

And how they responded as the campaign mileage piled up, particularly after the TV debates! One day as he rode in an open convertible through the coal regions of Pennsylvania with Governor David Lawrence of that state, through a score of sooty, bedraggled, clapboard towns, the crowds tore at his sleeves, bombarded him with flowers, seized his peeping French cuffs, and grabbed for his right hand until it became a puffy, bleeding, lacerated lump of flesh. The sun set and night fell over the cavalcade, by now hopelessly behind schedule. Between two towns, Kennedy changed cars at a gas station and stood ruefully inspecting his mangled right hand. He stared at it, with glazed eye, as though the hand no longer belonged to him at all. Then he swathed it in a handkerchief, shrugged and boarded another car. Governor Lawrence meanwhile exulted to newsmen: "They're worshiping him like a saint. Even Franklin Roosevelt never got that kind of crowd here. They love him!"

Above all, the dames loved him. Little girls with bare legs ran screaming alongside his car. Once a teenage girl touched his hand, then ran off in semihysteria crying "I touched him, I touched him," and at last fainted in another girl's arms. Middle-aged mothers bounced when Kennedy passed. Nuns in black habits waved wildly. These female partisans were classified by reporters as: teeterers, jumpers, lopers, bouncers, or leapers. In the press bus, a newsman would sing out the score in the last village: "fifteen jumpers, five bouncers, eighty-five leapers. This burg is mostly leapers."

It certainly wasn't Kennedy's campaign oratory that set them afire. His voice was high-pitched, thin, and usually hoarse; his words scarcely worth recording by historians. It became essentially a personality contest between himself and Richard Nixon—and a struggle by Kennedy to convince those Protestants suspicious that the Pope might wind up mentor of a Catholic President. In debates with Nixon he was at his best, alert, agile, brittle, disputatious, brimful of statistics—his plain, unadorned style seemed made for TV, not the stump.

He would, he said, get the "country moving again;" he said that American prestige was on the wane, that the G.O.P. was at fault, and he dwelt on those themes until the members of his entourage could put themselves to sleep by the cadence. He pictured the country as languishing, stagnant, a torpid giant without zest or gumption. He knew it was an exaggeration, but the outs must attack, and President Eisenhower hadn't left much room for an attacker to get a foothold.

His opening seldom varied. "I come to St. Louis (or Chicago, Lewiston, Newark, or San Antonio)" he would say, "because I think it's time that we get this country moving again." He shouted it in his curiously Boston-Harvard accent, leaving off r's where there were r's, and adding r's where there were none. On windy fall days there was a gutteral scratch to his voice. He stood there bareheaded, usually coatless, in his tailored two-button suit, French cuffs showing a snowy fringe above his wrists, and his right hand pumping in that queer characteristic gesture: thumb pressed against forefinger. He praised the Democratic party, mentioned his Republican opponents but rarely, and called his countrymen to toil and sacrifice for a better America. (Sample jibe at Nixon: "In the last seven days he has called me an ignoramus, a liar, a Pied Piper and, all the rest. I just confine myself to calling him a Republican . . . and he says that is really getting low."

The real Kennedy surfaced at the end of these open-air speeches when he usually quoted poetry, chiefly Robert Frost, then tacked on a bit of understated whimsy tending to deprecate himself and his big mission. At New York University, he reeled off some favorite lines from Robert Frost: "But I have promises to keep . . . And miles to go before I sleep . . . And miles to go before I sleep," and then quipped: "And now I go to Brooklyn."

(His brother Bobby, in his own New York Senatorial campaign, adapted one effective JFK technique: milking yes and no answers from the audience with a touch of laughter. "I ask you, was Senator Keating on the floor of the Senate when the Aid to Education bill was coming up?" Yelling audience: "No! No! No!" Robert Kennedy: "You're wrong, he *was*."

Candidate Kennedy was utterly disdainful of his own body in that exhausting grind of 1960, which left reporters and his entourage punchy-groggy. He still suffered painfully from the back operation that almost cost him his life a few years earlier, but he moved as though he were a reckless college boy in the bloom of physical fitness. He seldom opened the door of a convertible to get out. He threw his legs over the side and slid out. He stood up, instead of sitting down, while the car careened along. One night in Joliet, Illinois, when the press of the crowd hemmed in his convertible and brought it to a halt, he leaped over the hoods of three other cars to get to the speaker's platform.

Another night, crossing the bridge over the Mississippi River between Illinois and Iowa at Davenport, Kennedy walked from one car to another while both were moving. In Los Angeles one bright day, he vaulted over the side when the overheated motor of his convertible caught fire. One day, his helicopter pilot lost his way in the smog and had to put the Presidential candidate down in a vacant lot. At the Democratic convention in that city, to avoid newsmen, Kennedy left an apartment house and scaled a high alley fence to attend, unseen, a party at the home his father was renting.

His recuperative powers, like most good politicians, were superb. He could fall asleep in five minutes and often napped in the *Caroline* between cities. Several times he stretched out on the floors of planes and

fell asleep, wrapped in a blanket, undisturbed by the loud talk around him.

Throughout the campaign, John Kennedy fought to keep a delicate chemical balance, for Kennedy suffered from an insufficiency of the adrenal glands, a mild form of Addison's disease. He took regular medication for it and he occasionally joked about it. One frosty morning, while his cavalcade formed outside suburban Chicago's O'Hare Inn, he spotted a reporter who had written one of the few stories about his affliction. "You'll be happy today," said Kennedy with a taunting smile. "We're going through Addison this afternoon."

He ate constantly, like a child, on the campaign route. Where his brother Bobby wolfed huge bowls of chocolate ice cream and gobs of chocolate cake, Jack Kennedy drank quarts of milk, consumed endless bowls of specially prepared fish chowder, and munched away at sandwiches. Although he was sparing with hard liquor, he liked Heineken's beer and always had an ample supply aboard the *Caroline*.

In the last days of the campaign, taut but composed, he would prowl the *Caroline*, chatting with his sisters or the pool newsmen. The reporters would hide local newspapers picked up from the latest stop, for Kennedy was a newsprint thief. "Stick that paper behind you," the UPI's Merriman Smith would order a colleague, "Here comes the boy paper stealer." On the last day of the campaign, flying across Vermont, Kennedy snitched a last newspaper, scanned it hurriedly for news of Nixon and then answered questions. How did he really feel about the outcome of tomorrow's voting?

Completely detached, as though he were analyzing an election in Australia, Kennedy frowned and opined: "I think we'll win. But it will be a lot closer than some people think. Lou Harris (his pollster) shows me that much ahead." He made a small space with thumb and forefinger. "Nixon has come up some in the last two weeks. But there's nothing more we can do now. We've done our best and it's over tonight." His forecast, as usual where his own fortunes were concerned, was coldly accurate. The next day he received 118,550 votes more than Nixon, or less than 2/10s of 1 per cent of the 68,335,000 votes cast in the 50 states. When the last week's polls showed him slipping, he asked, "What is there about me that scares people in the last week of a campaign?"

Now neither staffers, newsmen, or plain citizens get quite the intimate picture of a Presidential candidate as do the photographers. The "regulars" who dog him day and night, men of the AP, UPI, magazines, and newsreels, ride in the Photo Car directly ahead of the Man or if the street is wide enough cruise abreast of his car. A notably ferocious, combative breed, their job at all costs is to get an unobstructed view of the candidate, in case an egg is tossed or something electric happens. With the photographers, the candidate is mentally relaxed, for he knows they will not report what he says. They may be greedy to snatch him in ridiculous poses, but they care not what terrible gaff he may make in speech or conversation. To them, the candidate is a body, not a mind.

In the guerilla tactics of the craft, outpushing, shoving, running, elbowing, and outconniving the competition, Stanley Tretick has few peers. He has the nerve of a Brinks bandit, the persistence of a nagging toothache. For fifteen years, he had bird-dogged Presidents, Presidential condidates, and pols of infinite variety as a Washington wire service photographer before UPI assigned him to cover the Kennedy campaign, from Labor Day Kick-off in Detroit, to wild end at Boston's Faneuil Hall, and election night in Hyannis.

Jacqueline Kennedy recalls the first moment she spied him. It was in Hyannis, just after the Democratic convention. As she rode in an open car with her triumphant husband, a madman with a camera sprinted alongside, scattering bodies left and right. "My God, who's that?" she asked her husband. "His days are numbered."

Tretick began his study of Kennedy, much as the hunter studies his prey, on January 2, 1960, when Kennedy announced formally that he was a candidate for the Democratic nomination for President of the United States. The setting was the Senate Office Building's high-ceilinged, marble caucus room. It was the usual Washington mob scene of sweating, pushing, yelling photographers, reporters, and TV cameramen. During the photo session, with demure Jacqueline at his side, the Senator appeared skittish and nervous. "How about smiling?" someone yelled. JFK objected politely. He said he had read somewhere, *The New Yorker* perhaps, that candidates seemed perpetually wreathed in smiles. Did they have to smile all the time? "That's okay, Senator," cracked cameraman George Tames of *The New York Times.* "Everybody doesn't read *The New Yorker.*"

Columnist Alsop came through with another bit of insider advice: "Two things made JFK nervous," he said. "Nuns and silly hats."

Early on the Hyannis golf links, Tretick personally learned another lesson about covering Kennedy: the direct approach, without deception, worked best. JFK played golf, but very quietly, for Ike's hours on the links had been a prime target of Democratic criticism. One day Tretick trailed Kennedy to a golf course and walked several hundred yards across the fairway to ask: could he snap a picture of the players?

"Did you walk all that way just to ask me that?" asked the astonished candidate. "You have a long lens. Why didn't you just photograph me from a distance?" No, it was a private game, explained Stanley, he wanted permission. That impressed JFK who respected the privacy of others and sought it for himself. But the answer was still no—words about his golfing were one thing, graphic photos another. All right, agreed Tretick, no golfing shot—but how about an exclusive session with his wife and Caroline? The reward for playing it straight was a family photo the next noon. Lesson 2: JFK respected enterprise and was a man with whom one could strike a bargain.

Lesson 3: the pally approach was definitely out. A reporter who had long been a personal friend of the Senator's after the nomination still kept on addressing him as "Jack" in on-the-air interviews, and it was apparent this nettled Kennedy. He was a United States *Senator,* and wished to be addressed by that title.

Since Tretick's sole preoccupation for two months would be Kennedy, he decided to approach him directly about his future assignment, on a plane winging back from Alaska.

The candidate, typically, expressed himself candidly about photographers in general. He was not terribly flattering, saying he thought he was a better judge of what he should pose for than most photographers he'd run across. After all, he remarked, "there are a lot of clods carrying cameras in this country."

No use arguing with that, thought Stanley, and then proposed a bargain: "I'm going to be covering you through the whole campaign. I'd like to know right off what you like and don't like. I'll never ask you to pose. I promise not to maneuver you into an awkward situation on purpose, but if you happen into one I'll snap it—because my competition will." Fair enough ground rules, agreed JFK: snap away, if the incident actually happened, he knew that was the way the game was played. By now well aware of Kennedy's "silly hat" syndrome, Tretick persisted: "You know somebody is going to plunk an Indian headdress on you sooner or later in a ceremony." That was his worry, said Kennedy.

So began The Game which JFK was to play lightheartedly, skillfully, with the adhesive swarm of cameramen along 44,000 miles of campaign trail. With the same ability he used to hop from one slippery convertible hood to another, he somehow craftily ducked out of camera range, when:

1. Combing that chestnut thatch of hair, which he did frequently. 2. Eating anything, especially the Howard Johnson hot dogs and ice cream for which he had a passion. 3. Donning foolish hats. 4. Kissing his wife. And as Alsop had predicted, nuns made him nervous, too. Though he waved graciously to these ladies who lined the motorcade routes and often stopped to chat with them, he was jumpy and sensitive when the cameras closed in. As hard as it may be to recall now, his Catholicism was a burning campaign issue, and he knew full well those pictures would not sit well in the Protestant Bible Belt.

In playing The Game, Kennedy was an amused, observant spectator of the fights and blasphemous wrangles that convulsed the riders of the photo car, directly ahead of his. The "regulars" guarded their staked-out, privileged positions against "local" cameramen who tried to clamber aboard with the ferocity of jungle fighters. He also kept tabs on the romances in that car—for pretty girls were as welcome aboard as local photographers were repelled. (Toward the groggy end of the campaign ordeal, two cameramen who'd gone the whole route rewarded their observant subject with a gift of their own. They bought a little model Stutz touring car of the 1920's, labeled it Photo Car, jammed it with toy figures, scotchtaping them to seats, fenders, hood—one even hung perilously from a back bumper. In his hotel suite, Kennedy unveiled the offering, swathed in a towel, and spying the poor wretch hanging from the bumper, asked, "Is that the local man?")

It was in Sioux Falls that Tretick heard that the unthinkable was about to happen. A tribal chief was set to crown Kennedy with an Indian war bonnet.

"I studied the speaker's stand, and perched in the best spot to get that shot. When Kennedy arrived he was nervous, God was he nervous. He knew what was coming, and it was killing him. Sure enough, as he stood there stiff as a poker, they plunked the feathers on him—but for only an eighth of a second. He slipped it off mumbling, 'Thanks very much,' but I'd gotten the picture and next day it was blown up three or four columns wide in the paper. It was silly looking. I sent it to Kennedy with a note 'You gotta be quick.' That gave him quite a charge; he laughed, 'Oh, we'll have better days.'"

Sometimes JFK lost the hat game, more times he won. In St. Louis an official plopped a cowboy hat on his head, but only for a fraction of a second. "Would you put that on again, sir?" the official asked, trying to be helpful. "I think those fellows over there missed the shot." Kennedy grinned at the photographers and said with relish: "I'm glad."

There again he was "hip"—most politicians couldn't care less who make what pictures, but somehow he kept track of credit lines, and if he liked a shot asked for a copy of it. He played the cat-and-mouse game skillfully, deviously, but when he lost and was nailed in an awkward pose, he didn't get into a lather about it. He solved the problem by dodging the situation altogether. In Minneapolis, a night club singer sought to publicize her act by giving Kennedy a huge Mexican sombrero. "I'll put it where it belongs," said Kennedy, promptly placing it on the head of Hubert Humphrey. His hat phobia inspired one of his funniest cracks, after the election, when he flew off to Texas to meet with his new vice president at Lyndon Johnson's ranch. LBJ came loping to meet the President-elect at the airport, a big Texas skimmer on his head. JFK took a long, quizzical look, then said: "Take off that silly hat."

Curiously, he would pose in one kind of headgear—a workman's hard hat. Not for long, but he did it. Perhaps he thought a refusal might affront the men in the granite quarries, the factories, and the mines he visited? "It was impressive," says Tretick, "the way working men, the kind who work at hard physical labor, went for Kennedy. What they saw in him, unlike the female jumpers and screamers, was the fighter, the competitor."

"Go get 'em, Big Boy," they'd yell. "Attaboy, Jack, you tell 'em." "Hiya Jackson old buddy."

In Sioux City, there was an atypical moment when he actually climbed on a horse. If photographers had barked out orders to do so, he wouldn't have in a thousand light years; but a stockyards workman dared: "I'll bet you can't ride that horse," (which was actually a white mule). Perhaps it was the frontal challenge, but he leaped nimbly aboard its back.

It was a lighthearted, skylarking campaign, and NBC-TV's Herb Kaplow, joining Kennedy after a sober stretch with the Republican candidate, observed: "Nixon's campaign is truth and purity. This one seems to be fun and frolic."

Nixon had the fixation that the press coverage was critical of him. Kennedy felt that reporters were his friends, or at worst, neutral. Both probably had good reason for their feeling. Kennedy, once a newsman himself, got along with the breed, and cultivated them. "To be transferred from the Nixon campaign tour to the Kennedy campaign tour meant no lightening of exertion or weariness for any newspaperman—but it was as if one were transformed in role from leper and outcast to friend and battle companion," wrote Theodore White in *The Making of a President*. If his set get-the-country-moving-again oratory left newsmen groggy, the "funnies" he pulled brightened the long day.

There was the time, when handed a watermelon that weighed 142 pounds, Kennedy recoiled in mock horror, and asked: "Is it still alive?"

In Tennessee, when Senator Albert Gore proudly showed off his prize bull at a livestock exhibit, candidate Kennedy peered at the animal and wondered: "Has he been getting much . . . uh . . . recognition lately?"

Pulling out of St. Louis in a motorcade, the air around the photo car suddenly seemed to be raining apples. Someone had given JFK a basket of fruit and Kennedy seemed to be testing his throwing arm. "We never knew," said one photographer, "whether he was trying to pelt us or feed us."

The duel between candidate and his posse of photographers went on and on. Just why a picture of a politician eating (or plonking a hat on his head) makes news is one of the mysteries of photojournalism; but Kennedy got through that campaign ducking both situations nine times out of ten.

Once the stalkers thought they had him cornered. He had ducked into a Howard Johnson's restaurant and come out with two hot dogs. They waited. He waited, then cracked: "Oh no you don't, not after that picture of Lodge, Lefkowitz, and Rockefeller," for he'd seen a shot of the three Republicans chomping on giant frankfurters at Coney Island. Holding the hot dogs low and out of sight, he clambered into his car, while photographers boarded theirs getting out their long lenses. He foiled them again by sliding down under the dashboard to eat his snack.

In Des Moines, Iowa, he seemed cornered for sure, when he was handed the inevitable ear of prize Iowa corn. He finessed that by snapping the huge ear in two, ruining the whole effect.

Photographed affection was also OUT. Once, in a jet from which he habitually deplaned via the front door, he dashed out the back to greet a waiting Jackie. There was a mad, wild scramble as photographers reverse-charged out the rear, yelling: "Kiss her again, Senator," "Hug him, Jackie," "Put your arm around her, Senator." Declining to carry out these bawled instructions, he stood bemused and said, "You're sure an affectionate group of photographers."

Kennedy's handling of the inevitable campaign hecklers varied widely with the type. Sometimes, if an issue were fairly raised, he'd give a serious reply. Often he'd merely nod and grin at the zealous Republican who interrupted his speech. He seldom got angry. If irritated, he could become coldly dismissive, as illustrated by an incident in New York State. All day long the motorcade had been dogged by a tough, gravel-voiced, beefy character, a Former West Coast Teamster. He passed out Nixon buttons and literature and shouted within earshot of the candidate about various iniquities visited on the Teamsters by the Kennedy brothers. When the cavalcade paused at a tollgate, the heckler swaggered up to the candidate's car while all eyes in the entourage followed his progress. Kennedy glared at him, and said: "Get lost, fatso." For some reason, that so unnerved the fellow he wandered off and was seen no more.

When he did become visibly angry, he kept that emotion under tight control. Once he was cruising through the outskirts of Milwaukee when a man, obviously drunk, threw his drink, glass and all, right at Kennedy. The liquid splashed his coat, the tumbler fell into the car. Kennedy reached down, retrieved the glass, and then handed it to the man, still teetering in the van of the crowd. "Here's your glass," said Kennedy. That was all.

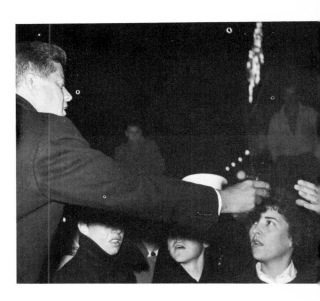

Near Scranton, Pennsylvania, the crowds nearly drowned the candidate and his convertible, but what caught Tretick's eye was a man, dancing solitarily in the street, juggling a bunch of bananas. It was clear that for some unfathomable reason he was set to throw it at Kennedy, and sure enough JFK caught it. By the time the motorcade pulled into Wilkes Barre, and Kennedy had departed for a rally, the bananas still sat on the floor of the car. Tretick plucked one and was eating it when two teenagers came up, and asked, almost reverently: "Is that a banana out of *Kennedy's* car?" "Can we please have the skins?" they begged.

"People who worked on the campaign had a common bond, as if they'd been through a war together," said "Fiddle," young Priscilla Wear. Indeed, Jacqueline Kennedy's prediction that Tretick wouldn't survive that war unscathed came true. Lagging behind a motorcade, to take a few street shots, he tried to catch up by climbing aboard the nearest moving vehicle, which promptly speeded up. In that pratfall, he cracked his chin and the bone in his left working hand. Next day, battle scarred, he showed up in bandage and cast, camera at the ready, to be greeted respectfully by JFK as "Our Veteran."

Mobs *per se* never much interested Kennedy, but individuals did. I know of no photographer or newsman who covered that campaign, start to finish, who didn't come away thinking he *knew* John F. Kennedy—they were no longer the press corps, but his friends. In turn, the President knew them and all their idiosyncracies.

When he moved into the White House, his highly personalized Oval Office, aclutter with mementos, there were the New England sailing ships, the stylish black alligator desk set, gift of President Charles De Gaulle—and a handsome leather photo album, set on a small table hard by his desk. It was the only one in the office, and his favorite pictorial record of that extraordinary campaign ordeal, which set a new style in Presidential campaigning. In it were fifty-seven pictures Tretick had culled from his coverage (of which fifteen are included in this book). It was his "Status Symbol," he used to say. The day it vanished, he reckoned, would be sure proof he was out of Presidential favor. There the album remained, until after November 22, and the day JFK's Presidential flags, his rocking chair, all the memorabilia of his presidency, left the White House.

Right: He learned a lot about the art of handshaking the hard way, after his right hand became bruised and swollen.

Above: The millions of females who screamed and bounced and jiggled at the very sight of JFK passing by couldn't know it, but their frenzied adulation more often bemused than elated their hero.

Left: The more reserved and restrained he was, the more they screamed out their affection, unrestrained.

Left: Near Scranton, Pennsylvania, a fan chucked a bunch of bananas at Kennedy for some unfathomable reason. JFK, an old pro at touch football, fielded this gift neatly.

Above: Getting out from under.

Below: Adept as he was at ducking "corny" pictures, it was inevitable that he would be caught with the traditional campaign baby.

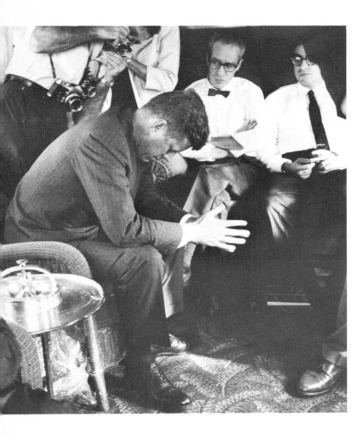

Above: Campaign strategy: aboard a train in California, the candidate and staff members John Bartlow Martin and Richard Goodwin confer about a major, upcoming speech.

Right and far right: His recuperative powers, like most good politicians', were superb. He could fall asleep in five minutes, and even napped on the floor of planes, flying between cities, unperturbed by the talk of reporters and staffers around him. "When in doubt," he once said on the Caroline, *"sleep."*

The jet-maniacal campaign was over at last, and on election morning JFK strolled up the beach at Hyannis Port, Caroline clasped in his arms. Fellow strollers included his aide Ted Sorensen, Edward Kennedy, Jean Smith, and Joan Kennedy.

The Caroline crisis

The heavyweight thinkers will dwell for years on major crises of the Kennedy Administration—the Bay of Pigs, Laos, the Steel Price Rise, Missiles in Cuba, Viet Nam. The antagonists of the young President were Communists and capitalists: giant size all, Castro, Khrushchev, Mao Tse-Tung, Roger Blough. And me.

For smack in the middle was a featherweight crisis that seemed to absorb almost as much of JFK's time and energy as a global confrontation. Locked in the struggle were prestigious institutions; the White House, *Look* magazine, the Presidency, the Press.

For his side of the combat, President Kennedy marshaled a kind of "Excom" board of strategy, as he did in the Cuban missile crisis. His brother Bobby was a member, a tower of strength for this doll-house war, just as he was for such headline showdowns as missiles, steel, and Cuban invasions. Press Secretary Pierre Salinger, the merry fat man with the big cigar, played a role as embattled as Secretary of Defense Robert S. McNamara on other war fronts. Various members of the White House secretariat were dragooned into the act.

The prize of war was a tawny-haired, three-year-old child, the President's daughter Caroline. The *casus belli* was primitive and elemental, much easier to understand than complex economic or ideological issues: A big magazine wanted to print intimate pictures of Caroline. Jacqueline Kennedy did not want the pictures printed.

Jackie, in truth, was the chief protagonist, an embattled mother with an instinctive brood sense for protection of her young. The President was, at first, a hesitant warrior, pressed into service by his wife. But once he realized her maternal ire was aroused, he assumed command of the troops in her name.

JFK came to the combat well armed, for he knew as much about the intricacies of journalism as the reporters who covered him. Fresh in office, he was asked about an irreverent magazine profile of himself. "Well," he replied, "the text was okay, but I didn't much care for the sell lines." The "sell lines," or headlines for the article, had blared: "He bears grudges. He doesn't enjoy mobs. He cusses freely. He drives too fast. He's seldom on time."

Perhaps because of his newspaper background and his long friendship with many journalists, Kennedy's honeymoon with the press was a lengthy one. But eventually his all-seeing eye and instant reaction to anything printed about him or his administration became the problem. The senior White House correspondent, Merriman Smith of United Press International, put it thus: "Every administration develops Potomac sunburn sooner or later. The main difference with the Kennedy people is that their hypersensitivity developed so early. One reason is the close attention they pay to everything written about them. How they can spot an obscure paragraph in a paper of 3,000 circulation 2,000 miles away is beyond me. They must have a thousand little gnomes reading the papers for them."

That was the setting in which the great Caroline Crisis was born. And like most of the New Frontier crises, this one was fought out largely in private, away from the thundering headlines of Page One.

At three, Caroline so resembled JFK that she even walked like him with hunched, forward-thrust shoulders, hands jammed in her pockets. Her talkativeness prompted JFK's reply to a Congressman who remarked that his own daughter had said she wouldn't want to live in the White House: "That's not my trouble with Caroline. My problem is to keep her from holding press conferences."

Caroline was a natural news target. Republicans looked upon her as JFK's secret weapon for re-election in 1964. All America clamored to see her. On a day when 13,000 tourists had gone through the newly refurbished White House, a five-year-old girl was spotted in a downpour of tears. She had seen the Red Room and the Blue Room, but she wailed inconsolably to her mother: "I want to see Caroline."

For the under-ten set, Caroline was the new Shirley Temple, inspiring fan mail which ran to sixty letters a day. Comic books about her were snapped up by pre-teenage readers.

She also inspired some of Salinger's more bizarre press briefings. Sample: "Q. Pierre, are you kidding? Has she got a cat? A. I'm not kidding. Q. Is it really true that the cat has a hernia?" When Caroline's hamsters went AWOL in the White House, that was news. Through a top White House leak, one writer dug out the sensational murder story: the lady hamster had eaten her husband. It was news again when a live rabbit arrived for her. It was named Zsa Zsa and, reputedly, it drank beer and could play the first five bars of the "Star-Spangled Banner" on a trumpet. Later this moth-eaten vaudeville character was given away to an orphanage.

In the vortex of this public interest, the firm-willed Mrs. Kennedy sought to shield the children. If the public desire for Kennedy reading material was voracious, Mrs. Kennedy's original failure to comprehend it was profound. With wonderment in a TV interview, Jackie made the understatement of the year: "People seem so interested in what the First Family does." Was it possible to raise a child "normally" in the White House, she was asked. "I hope it is," she replied. "I'm trying very hard." Thus far, she said, she'd observed no big changes in her daughter. "She's too little, but I hold my breath about the day she goes to kindergarten. We treat her just the same. It's how other people treat her that's important."

In the battle for Caroline's privacy there came the early Planting-Of-The-Shrubs skirmish. On a fine spring day a new sandbox and swings

were installed on the White House South Lawn. When Caroline ran out to play, photographers with long lenses already were lining the high iron fence. Tourist buses promptly unloaded their cargoes of excited sight-seers. The scene resembled Sunday afternoon at the zoo. Alerted by Mrs. Kennedy, a distraught, pale-faced Pamela Turnure streaked into Salinger's office, begging: "Somebody do something, please!" The mansion went into action. Overnight a thicket of leafy rhododendrons was planted the length of the fence to shield the playground from public gaze. Salinger stoutly maintained that the shrubbery had been installed merely as a landscape-improvement scheme. The Washington *Star* taunted Salinger in a lengthy exposé of the foliage ruse. Little Caroline unknowingly had strewn ground glass in the honeymoon suite of Press and President.

It was in this setting that photographer Stanley Tretick went to Hyannis on Cape Cod one fine summer weekend to shoot informal photos of Sargent Shriver, chief of the newly hatched Peace Corps, and his family. That was all Tretick honestly had in mind—when he arrived.

The Kennedy compound at Hyannis had grown with the years. First Ambassador Joe Kennedy bought a rambling, clapboard, weatherbeaten seventeen-room house with wide New England porches to provide summer shelter for his expanding brood of children. Later, a few hundred feet away, his grown son Jack bought a modest house, comfortable but unpretentious. Bobby acquired a third house.

The three old homes fronted a large, smooth, billiard-green lawn that sloped into dune grass before plunging to the sands of the beach. It was a "triffic" place for kids, said Attorney General Kennedy of this 4.7 acres of family compound. A six-foot cedar fence blocked prying eyes from witnessing the tumultuous play of the swarming Kennedy cousins, offspring of six Kennedy marriages.

As Tretick waited for the Shrivers to appear, into his field of vision trotted little Caroline in quest of more cousins to play with. Her little-girl appeal was instant. She wore a terrycloth suit, Japanese sandals, and she sported sunglasses worn rakishly upside down. She was clutching a picture postcard of her father.

The picture was irresistible and Tretick snapped it with an automatic, professional reflex. Then he shot another and another as Caroline fell into an argument with cousin Maria Shriver over the man on the picture postcard. Maria pointed to the picture and loudly proclaimed, "That's the President." "No, no, it is not," Caroline argued hotly. "That's my Daddy!" With all her cousins, Caroline was just another Kennedy child, no rank puller or ringleader of the clan. She merited equal discipline too. As a sample, on a family sailing picnic with the Shrivers that day, when she strewed the boat bottom with peach pits, the Attorney General rebuked her sharply: "Caroline, will you please stop spitting in the boat."

By the end of the day's shooting, pictures of the Shrivers and Caroline were hopelessly intermingled on Tretick's film. Then Jacqueline came riding by in the Presidential golf cart, with her husband and his father. She was clearly upset to see a man with a camera. "You're not here to photograph us?" she asked dubiously. Pause. "Or Caroline either?" Tretick shook his head. No, he vowed, he was here to film the Shrivers.

Later, when Mrs. Kennedy learned of the pictured sailing picnic with Caroline aboard, she requested, via Pam Turnure, that Tretick swear a blood oath that Caroline would not appear in any of the Shriver picture sequences. Her plea was reinforced by a stern Attorney General. The middle-sized Kennedy brother broached Tretick and demanded that he take full responsibility for seeing that no Caroline pictures were printed. Absolutely, said Tretick.

But we were both battling human nature. Once the pictures were developed and went the rounds at *Look*, there was no containing the editors. These pictures were much too charming to go unpublished. Here was the President's daughter at her most natural—not posed artificially, or tricked out in her Sunday best, but just a wind-blown, tousle-haired, even grubby little three-year-old having a marvelous summer by the sea.

The President loved candid photos of his children. He couldn't get enough of them. Perhaps these might so beguile him that the White House could be persuaded to relax, just this once, the iron ban against Caroline shots. So, in due time, bent on this lowly editorial mission, with picture album tucked under an arm, I returned to the West Wing of the White House to make an impassioned pitch to Salinger. Better talk to the President about them, he said. The President? My reaction was incredulous as always. Why bother him with such trivia? But, then again, others did, so why not?

It was a lazy Friday afternoon. Washington boiled with heat and even the hyperkinetic White House was relaxed in July torpor. With his family at the Cape, JFK was a weekday summer bachelor and often worked afternoons in the cool, spacious family living quarters. I was to see him there, just before the chopper whirled him off on the first leg of the trip to Hyannis.

No corner of the White House seemed to be off-limits for writers in these early months. Journalists had invaded the swimming pool, the movie projection room and even the Presidential bedroom when invited. Talking while pursuing some other activity was the President's idea of saving time.

A private elevator, with walnut paneling and rich brown carpeting, carries visitors to the family apartments on the second floor. There one could

rubberneck, peering into the living room whose ambiance of informal elegance undeniably spelled Jacqueline. Chandeliers glittered overhead, the walls were pale yellow. A rocking chair rested by the fireplace, French chairs were grouped on the off-white rug along with a handsome, impractical, French empire desk.

JFK was closeted in a study, which like his bedroom, opened on the long hall that swept the width of the house. In the waiting area, the wall held American Indian prints by George Caitlin that had been borrowed from the Smithsonian Institution.

Ralph Dungan, long-time Kennedy lieutenant, sat waiting too, leafing through the *New Republic,* staple fare among New Frontiersmen. From behind a closed door came a steady murmur of voices, one unmistakably Boston-Irish-Harvard-cum-New England. Occasionally a word like "Cuber" or Laos would smite the ear.

Suddenly the door swung open and out burst the President in shorts and shirt tail. He yelled down the hall: "Hey, Bundy, get me a Coke." Could that be McGeorge Bundy, that starchy, proper Bostonian and the Khan of national security affairs, a man whose ordinary conversation ran to words like "apocalyptic" and "sententious?" Spying me, JFK called out merrily: "Hi, Laurer. With you in a minute. How do you like the place?" He sounded as though he had just moved into some new digs in Georgetown.

The helicopter was already squatting on the South Lawn by the time Kennedy was dressed and ready to talk. He leafed through the album of Caroline pictures, pausing to admire an occasional frame and remarking that these were the kind of pictures *he* liked.

I made my pitch to print the Caroline pictures, knowing he was a reasonable man open to persuasion, particularly in matters of self-interest. I argued that the pictures did not present her as a privileged President's daughter, but as any ordinary American kid. The Kennedy White House was renowned for its elegance and gloss, but these pictures of his daughter were such *human* pictures. Could he persuade his wife to lift the no-Caroline ban? He could make no promises, he said, because Jackie's word was law in such family matters, but he would give it a try that weekend.

Then, putting aside the album, he said: "Tell me about your friend Guevara." Guevara? Guevara? Good Lord.

On my last trip to Cuba, I'd interviewed this Argentine doctor turned Cuban revolutionary and guerilla warfare specialist. But to shift gears suddenly from Caroline and sum up Guevara for a President was a large order. I tried. Guevara was cool, brainy, blunt, witty, sensible, I said. Where Castro was the revolutionary, flammable orator roaming the countryside, Guevara was the pragmatic Marxist, an enemy to be reckoned with. Great appeal for Latin youth. Indeed, I added, if they hadn't been polar opposites politically, Guevara and JFK were not unlike each other.

Kennedy at the time, it was revealed later, was reading heavily in guerilla warfare, including tomes by Guevara, Mao Tse Tung, and even a log of the Irish Republican army. He was pondering the problem, not of coping with the Big Bomb wars, but the nagging, guerilla skirmishes plaguing Latin America and Southeast Asia.

The President asked more abrupt, peppering questions, the skillful reportorial kind in which he picked his interviewer's brains without divulging what he thought. Then, taking a puff on his cigar, he leaned back and gave me a quizzical, appraising look.

"Something," he said lightly, "gives me the feeling you've got the hots for the 'Che.'"

If he meant to shake me up, he succeeded. It wasn't simply the fact of such hip lingo coming from a President, but his nettling implication that a reporter's professional faculties had been muddled by a subject's charm. Was he serious or needling? "Mr. President," I sputtered, "that was an odd remark." He had asked for a critical appraisal of a hotly controversial political figure, and I wasn't the only reporter who had a grudging respect for Guevara. The feeling was shared even by Cuban exiles who loathed the Castro regime. My strange 2:30 A.M. interview with Guevara had been more like a session of two wary antagonists than journalist and subject, I said. Hadn't the President seen the picture of me and the coil-eyed Che having a fierce exchange?

He puffed again on his cigar and gave me another amused look with hooded eyes. "Yeah," said JFK drily, "but you know what psychiatrists say . . . that kind of hostility often leads to an opposite emotion."

While I floundered for a telling rebuttal, he tucked the Caroline album under his arm and started for the elevator and the waiting helicopter. Would I like to tag along and watch the take-off? Sure, I'd be delighted to wave good-bye. Perhaps, I said, that was my problem, the girl left behind always waving good-bye.

"Laurer," was his parting shot. "I don't think *that's* your problem."

Whatever the vigor of his intercessions with Jackie that weekend on the Caroline pictures, they were futile. "My wife is a very strong woman," he said once. The result of all this high-level negotiating was that Mrs. Kennedy approved use of only one picture: Caroline standing on the Hyannis lawn, butterfly net in hand, but *back* to the camera. Jackie sent word that a rear view of her child wasn't so objectionable. By her logic, it helped preserve her daughter's anonymity. She'd once even voiced the forlorn hope that her children would be able to walk out of the White House unrecognized in 1965.

Then in the mails came a thoughtful, handwritten note from her, frankly spelling out her problem: "So many thanks for the marvelous pictures in the album . . . You are right—they are such good pictures . . .

It is partly because they are so good I must sadly tell you I just can't give you permission to publish them. Caroline was being recognized wherever she went. That is a strange enough thing to get used to at any age—but pretty sad when one is only three. Every article just increases the interest in her—her little friends and cousins see it and mention it to her and it is all bad for her—For the first time since the election things have abated a bit as far as she is concerned—and it has made me so happy. I must keep it that way. If I had known her picture would be taken that day I would never have let her go on the sailing picnic. I'm sure you can understand my feelings—as an editor it is difficult, but as a person I know you will because the article you did about me was so full of understanding . . . Gratefully, Jacqueline Kennedy."

I sympathized with her completely, cursing the day Caroline ever wandered in front of the camera. But there was a new problem now. The pictures had stirred interest for a story on Caroline, and since the pictures were forbidden, the magazine space would have to be filled by words alone. Whatever did one write about a three-year-old child, anyway, particularly one whose mother pleaded to keep her out of the news?

It was a professional dilemma, and JFK, the editorial expert, came up with some useful ideas, suggesting an interview with the Secret Service agents who guarded his daughter. A member of this "diaper detail" herded young Kennedys, whom he called "My Indians," to the West Side Beach Club or to the family's nearby rented farm for a day of riding. Cornering one agent, I asked whether it were true, as former Secret Service Chief U.E. Baughman had written, that guardians of Presidential children were an elite corps selected because they were "particularly good with children and sensitive to their needs?"

The agent must have had a bad day, for he replied deadpan: "My pet peeves—in this order—are kids, dogs, cats, and horses."

Muggsy O'Leary wasn't much more helpful. Asked if Caroline realized her father's position, he replied: "She don't know whether her pop's the President of the United Shoe Factory or the U.S. of A."

"How's it coming?" asked JFK, the sympathetic collaborator, during a casual encounter in Hyannis. Just then Caroline herself trotted up, dripping wet from a swim.

"Caroline," asked her father, "would you like to meet this nice lady?"

Miss Kennedy clasped her arms, gave me a long, cool stare and tendered me a one-word interview.

"No," she said.

"But Caroline," I pleaded, "I'm your *biographer*."

She continued to stare in silence. Her mother had trained her well. There would be no racy tidbits of life among the Kennedys from Miss Caroline.

All this fluff went into the Caroline profile along with such historic facts as her excellent performance as a trampoline bouncer, her horsemanship, and her sailing. She doted on French records and she kissed cats, although her pet Tom Kitten had been shipped away from the White House because the lawn was too big for him to roam on. If these words won no Pulitzer Prize, neither did they fetch any loud hosannas from Mrs. Kennedy. The piece was discussed on a flight from Washington to Hyannis. The President liked it. Sorensen liked it. Salinger liked it; she was told by Sorensen who asked what did she think? "That doesn't say much for your literary judgment," Mrs. Kennedy informed him.

Caroline was profiled, but unfortunately not forgotten.

The lady kept blossoming all over the public prints, in words as sticky as mine and with photographs ancient and new. There were galleys of type and bundles of pictures about the children's birthdays, their dogs, their presents. *The New York Times* at Halloween reported that Caroline had gone trick-or-treating in Georgetown. New York editors queried Pamela Turnure for information about how the girl would be wearing her hair next spring—as a guide to girls aged four to ten, please.

A year rolled round and the Tretick pictures taken in Hyannis had become veritable antiques. Caroline was four now and much changed. Once more the editors decided to ask Mrs. Kennedy for permission to publish the outdated photos. So back to the White House went Caroline's biographer to mingle her problem with those of Big Steel, Berlin, Laos, and Cuba. Charming girl, this Caroline, but one was staggered by how many hours of White House and editorial time were being expended on her public relations.

There was no use badgering Mrs. Kennedy. She was remote and calm in her quarters—as unapproachable as the President was accessible. Pressed to reopen *l'affaire* Caroline, Pierre Salinger muttered vaguely that he'd give it a try, but he was obviously more engrossed in other pressing matters of state. As so often happened when a mission was entrusted to Salinger, nothing happened. Weeks dragged by with no definite yes or no from the White House. Then, for a variety of editorial reasons, including the fact that Caroline pictures were appearing elsewhere, *Look's* editors took the plunge and printed the year-old intimate shots of Caroline under the title, "Caroline's Wonderful Summer."

The White House shook to its timbers the day the issue hit the newsstands. The President's Irish temper boiled and in sulphurous language he ordered: "Get that so-and-so Tretick on the phone." Luckily at that hour, 7 P.M., Stanley was shopping in a supermarket and missed the royal dressing-down. "It's lucky you weren't around when the President saw those pictures," Sorensen told him later. I wandered into the White House West Lobby to pick up baggage after a Hyannis trip. Salinger spied me and gave chase, roaring, "You'll never get another story out of *This* White House." Attorney General Kennedy took the position that security had been breached, as serious a matter as though the enemy had broken a top secret U.S. military code. "My father always said you'd use those pictures," he said bleakly. Bobby nagged at the subject for months and one began to get a compassionate feeling for Jimmy Hoffa.

The President's own wrath was short-lived. Actually, he was tickled by the pictures of his daughter. "He loved them," said Kenneth O'Donnell. The only picture the President disliked was the one in which Caroline held up his picture. JFK deemed that one corny and contrived. Mrs. Kennedy objected to those showing her daughter arguing with cousin Maria Shriver because they made Caroline look "bratty," she thought.

Unpardonable in the Kennedy family's book had been the breaking of a trust. Word had been pledged that the pictures would not appear, yet they did. The Kennedys cared not for ameliorating circumstances, including the prime competitive fact that other publications were sprouting with Caroline pictures. Even JFK's normally acute editorial instinct seemed to leave him in this case. Tretick and I were treated by him with the cold, steely look, despite the fact he'd liked the pictures. But his overt displeasure infected the staff down to the lowliest secretary. Reproachful looks were plentiful. Eventually, of course, diplomatic relations were restored, as they always are after the cessation of hostilities. When I called on the President some weeks later, Salinger ushered me in with the remark: "Don't be scared. We don't have machine guns behind the door."

The brouhaha seems, in retrospect, to be much ado about nothing. But it pointed up a number of things about the Kennedys. They did not care to be crossed. Also, once they flung the door of the White House wide for special stories, they expected fair treatment in return, a practice that led to the "managed news" outcry from suffering Republicans. But perhaps more significantly, the Caroline crisis proved that the Kennedys were very human. It is an old adage of photographers that prominent people love to see themselves and their families in pictures, provided the pictures are good, no matter what protestations to the contrary have been made. The Kennedys were no exception to the rule. The Caroline pictures became prized items in the family gallery.

Hair tousled and bundled up in a terry robe, Caroline comes home after a Kennedy family sailing picnic.

*Above: Young seafaring Kennedys aboard the sailboat
Victura: Michael Kennedy, son of the Attorney General, Caroline,
and her special buddy, cousin "Stevie" Smith, Jr.*

*Right: The breezy front porch of Ambassador Kennedy's house
was the best place on the compound for Kennedy-watching.*

Cousinly argument:
"This is the President," said Maria Shriver.
"No," Caroline objected. "That's my Daddy."
"But he's the President too," countered Maria.
"No, No, that's my Daddy."

Right: Clan-gathering in Hyannis Port: Ambassador Joseph Kennedy, the family patriarch, and the Sargent Shrivers.

Far right: Sandy, the children's "physics" instructor, balanced fearless Maria Shriver on the palm of one hand while her father Sargent Shriver looked on, equally fearless.

Below: Caroline on a family sailing picnic with the Shrivers.

Right: Hyannis Port. Alas, of many charming pictures of Caroline taken that weekend, this is the lone one Mrs. Kennedy approved. Her reasoning: it showed her daughter from the back and thus helped preserve Caroline's anonymity—or did it?

Below: The nation's Number 1 girl child, on the way to meet her cousins, stands solo on the dock fronting the Kennedy compound. Note one Presidential touch: the white phone, to the left, available for coping with instant crises.

Left to right: A gaggle of young Kennedys: Michael Kennedy, Steve Smith, Jr., Maria Shriver, and Caroline.

Uncle Jack
and the golf cart

The White House is a strange curse within a blessing for its occupants. No matter what toil and sacrifice a President undergoes to obtain the precious address, 1600 Pennsylvania Avenue, he is no sooner installed in the people's great white mansion than he begins to feel caged by the place.

Franklin D. Roosevelt fled it for long Hyde Park weekends. Harry Truman, viewing the White House as a "jail," flew back to Kansas City at every excuse, or relaxed in wild sports shirts in Key West, Florida. Dwight Eisenhower sought refuge in Gettysburg, or the golf links and clubhouse of Augusta, Georgia. Lyndon Johnson yearns openly for his Texas ranch, complaining that the roar of overhead planes and the clatter of tourists on the first floor thwarts sleep and peace of mind.

John F. Kennedy was no exception. As soon as spring brought the scent of blossoms to the land and it became good sailing weather, he itched to be off for the tang and mists of Cape Cod and the boisterous companionship of the Kennedy family compound. Hyannis, said a staffer, meant "freedom and liberation" for the President, a place where he could wear sneakers and polo shirt and conduct the nation's business between sailing picnics and expeditions with gaggles of small Kennedys.

The exodus from Washington began late Friday afternoon when three helicopters would rise in rotation from the White House back lawn, their blades whipping up winds that bent the magnolia trees and their clatter drowning the conversation of the Presidential retinue. Aides, Secret Service men, relatives, communications specialists, and even the unobtrusive guardian of the nation's atomic codes all clambered into the whirly-birds, in the Presidential entourage. They racketed clumsily to Andrews Air Force Base, in suburban Maryland, where the party transferred to a jet for the brief hop to Cape Cod. Then another transfer to helicopters for the final leg to the lawn of the Kennedy compound.

The best place to view the tumultuous arrival was the big, breezy front porch of Ambassador Joseph Kennedy's house overlooking Nantucket Sound. A visit there, any time, was filled with Kennedy Happenings. Bobby might be heard consoling a sobbing child. Or brother-in-law Sargent Shriver, the Peace Corps boss, would be instructing a swarm of Kennedy cousins in the art of wielding a baseball bat. Or, Pat Lawford, the President's sister, and wife of the movie actor, would come riding downhill crouched in a kid's coaster wagon. She braked the wagon and looked up to ask: Was the Yachtsman Motel really such a noisy, swinging place as rumored, with all those press types caged up there? And what about the funny lines in that night club skit that spoofed the Kennedys? Summers that compound bulged with some twenty Kennedy cousins, plus assorted friends. ("And that's only the beginning of the new Kennedys," said Muggsy

O'Leary. ("You need an adding machine to count those kids.") Kids bounced on the beach-front trampoline, whacked at baseballs, turned somersaults, chased butterflies, bounded into the ocean with appalling energy. Apart from the electric sight of the Presidential chopper whirling in on the weekend, the scene was livened by dogs, toys, maids, nurses, and young crewcut Secret Service men who lounged in bushes or sat in beach chairs facing out to sea, presumably on the lookout for Cuban invaders.

Debarking from his helicopter, the President made for his room and a quick change into sports clothes. Then he would scoop up Caroline and assorted nieces and nephews and wheel off in the golf cart to the local candy emporium two blocks away. "Friday evening he's a regular," reported owner Bob Garbutt. "He isn't down in the chopper fifteen minutes before he's over here." The President's orders: "Give the kids what they want." Then he'd fall to leafing through magazines on the newsstands while young Kennedys called out for licorice, chocolates, and "sugar daddies," the five-cent lollipops. His two-month bill for newsprint and goodies ran to $70. Meanwhile photographers with long lenses lurked blocks down the cordonned-off street, hoping to snap the golf cart before darkness closed in.

Muggsy O'Leary once said that "nobody loves kids like Bob and the Boss." All the Kennedys had a tribal way with children, but Uncle Jack was *it* for the little Kennedys—and not because he was the President, an eminence which some of them comprehended only vaguely. He was the bona fide Pied Piper uncle. One smart clap of his hands, as he boarded the golf cart bound for the ocean-front dock and a day of sailing, and every junior Kennedy able to walk materialized out of nowhere—streaking out of bushes and houses, deserting the trampoline and butterfly-chasing. They yelled as they ran, "Jack! Jack! Jack!" Once when Uncle Bobby banged up a cart fender in reckless driving, the little JFK partisans chanted, "We're going to tell Uncle Jack on you."

The President could be sitting in his sunny Hyannis living room, engrossed in adult talk with Shriver, or being briefed by his military aide, Maj. Gen. Chester V. (Ted) Clifton, when from two to a dozen children would tear in, bursting with the latest news about dogs, boats, and tribal mayhem. "Now, is that a fact," Kennedy would say, tendering them total, fascinated attention. He would poke them in the ribs and they'd giggle. The compound always crackled when Uncle Jack was in residence. He would dream up races, pairing off cousins by age, in which everyone seemed to win a prize. One four-year-old outsider, son of David Hackett, an assistant to Attorney General Kennedy, once hitched a ride to the Cape in *Air Force One*, then solemnly pronounced his judgment on his fellow passenger: "I *like* that President."

JFK's golf cart rides seemed to appeal more than everything else to

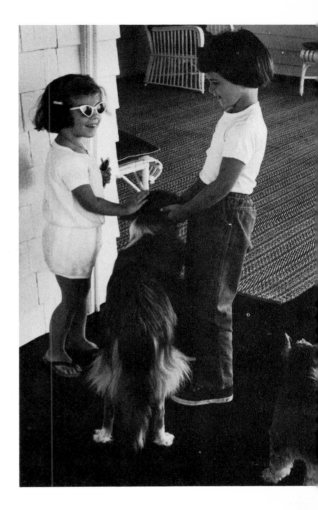

the children. My first view of this phenomenon came from the Ambassador's front porch where I had nearly punctured myself by sitting on a chair on which someone had left a spiked horseshoe. Photographer Stanley Tretick was with me. Within sight, by actual count, were eight bikes; two babies, one in a buggy and another crawling in the grass; three nannies in crisp white uniforms.

Then a white golf cart came whizzing by at such speed, it blurred before the eyes. The cart overflowed with minor Kennedys—were there six, eight, or ten?—but there was no mistaking the Kennedy at the wheel who wore knockabout clothes and sunglasses. It was the President.

First impression: His driving hadn't changed with his office. As a Senator and as a candidate, he drove his gray Oldsmobile convertible like a Grand Prix racer. He zoomed in and out of rush-hour traffic, ran red lights, and screeched around corners while chatting as pleasantly as though he were safe in an armchair at home. His passengers closed their eyes and prayed, ignoring the speedometer reading. Only two persons seemed unfazed by this hair-blown Barney Oldfield. One was Kenneth O'Donnell, whose emotional thermometer usually read below freezing anyway. The other was a serene Jacqueline who never seemed ruffled by her husband's vehicular near misses.

Now the President zoomed the golf cart up, down, and around the rolling compound hills, roller coaster style. The kids waved, laughed, and shrieked their pleasure while their nannies on the sidelines looked as nervous as Nixon in his first Kennedy debate. Of course, I instantly thought: What a great picture. And I could tell by the look on Stanley Tretick's face that two less-than-great minds had had the same thought.

Braking to a halt in front of the porch, JFK called out: "Hi Stanley, triffic pictures." (Of his daughter Caroline.) Then: "Hi, Laurer, what are you doing here? Why aren't you with your buddy?"

"Buddy?" I asked. What Buddy?

"Your buddy, the Che."

The President palavered about Guevara, who at the time was dueling Kennedy's emissaries at the Inter-American Conference at Punta del Este in Uruguay. What did the U.S. delegation report about Guevara, I asked. "He's getting fat," was the JFK news bulletin.

The kids were yelling for more thrills. "Hop aboard, Stanley," invited the President and away Tretick bounced, barely hanging on. But Tretick was ever the man of business. How about photographing this thing? he asked. Why not? replied the President. It was as simple as that. The seemingly impossible project was usually easy if he were approached directly—and he liked the idea. Check Mrs. Lincoln for a date soon, Kennedy added. One condition: No Caroline in the picture, although his daughter customarily rode in a privileged position on his lap. Caroline was taboo.

And so, arrangements made, we returned on another summer weekend to take the golf cart pictures and to record the auxiliary sound effects for a *Look* story. Again we perched on the Ambassador's porch, waiting for JFK to return from an ocean cruise.

The cruise, parenthetically, was another Hyannis ritual. Whether brilliant sunshine or muffling fog, on the appointed day, a file of servants could be seen trooping down to the dock with picnic baskets. The President would embark on the *Honey Fitz* with his wife and, usually, such relaxing friends as Paul (Red) Fay, an old PT-boat buddy who was now Under Secretary of the Navy, or Lem Billings, a family friend who knew all the labyrinthine Kennedy gossip. Or a visiting publisher, such as Philip Graham of the *Washington Post*, or a VIP, such as Adlai Stevenson, the U.N. Ambassador, might be aboard. Stevenson, indeed, even got a ride in the golf cart, and had been spied laughing his head off while clasping a bulging brief case to his chest. Graham one day found himself swimming in the ocean with the President 20 yards from the boat and wondering if such deep-sea sport wasn't a bit dangerous. Often as not, the *Honey Fitz's* captain didn't know his heading until the President clambered aboard and gave the destination. JFK would zip through newspapers, sun himself on deck, swim, and have a clam chowder lunch while the Secret Service patrolled in circling jet-powered motorboats to protect him from casual boaters and the ever-hovering photographers with long lenses who chartered their own craft in hopes, at least, of getting a picture of Jackie water-skiing.

That day, around 4 P.M., we idly watched as the yacht pulled into the dock and the party debarked. Then, to our dismay, we saw that Jacqueline Kennedy was boarding the golf cart with the children. She would be less than delighted to spy us again, the compound crashers, for even the Secret Service men roused the ire of the privacy-oriented Mrs. K when they trailed her on walks down Hyannis Beach. "You keep doing that," she once told them in her soft-iron way, "and you'll drive me right into the asylum." The gumshoes, who now ran to more compatible, discreet Ivy League types, did their best to remain near-invisible. But we were something else. She would bridle when she saw us, and probably—who knew—she would blow our arrangements sky-high with one emphatic word to her husband.

Tretick and I both panicked. He had wrestled tough Russian photographers in Vienna and I had brazened out a grilling by Cuban secret police, but now we ran down the wooden steps and scuttled out of sight behind the porch. Mrs. K has since been told that wars, firing lines, and other professional hazards paled by comparison to the terror she struck in our hearts. She is amused now, but she definitely would not have been then.

We cowered out of sight, until she'd been driven safely home. Back wheeled JFK alone in the golf cart. The cart was soon filled with as many screaming junior Kennedys as the cart could hold. Grinning his enjoyment, he circled the ambassadorial flag pole full throttle and wheeled up and down hill. Tretick rushed about the lawn like a madman, trying to track the cart and remember light, focus, and timing all at once. Then the President suddenly wheeled and came bearing down head-on at Tretick. Stanley stood his ground with the nervous bravado of a bullfighter and was missed by inches. All Kennedys went in for strenuous sports.

Later, the Kennedy entourage gathered at a party thrown by Larry Newman, a neighbor who lived catty-corner from JFK's house. The President strolled over to spend twenty minutes or so. An agog Canadian girl, squired to the cocktail hour by a Secret Service agent, was introduced to Kennedy. "Oh, Mr. President," she burbled, "I saw you in church yesterday and you're much more handsome than your pictures." As the President left, he tossed a slight wave of the hand at her and called: "See you in church."

But other guests were not beguiled by the Presidential presence. A President, no matter what his politics, would seem to be pretty heady stuff for a casual summer party. But not in these conservative precincts. Newman was a staunch friend, but many of the other Hyannis locals had never been comfortable so close to the Kennedys, the first Irish to invade Hyannis more than thirty years before. It riled old families in the summer of 1960 when hordes of newsmen, staff, and curiosity seekers boiled through the quiet corners of *their* town. They had even asked that Hyannis Port be totally sealed off from the public, an imperious request the police rejected as "impossible."

The party chatter at Newman's after the departure of the President ranged from patronizing to glowering comments from this John Birch Madras jacket set. After all, he was only old Jack Kennedy whom they'd known as a kid and who grew up to be a wild-eyed Democratic radical. But wasn't it gracious of a President to drop in on an old friend, one wasp-tongued lady was asked? Well, she sniffed, "At least Jack had the decency not to bring Arthur Schlesinger, Jr."

Later, back at JFK's house, we stood in the driveway with the President discussing such pressing matters as the golf cart, Caroline, and the Madras jacket set. Typically he wanted to know what had gone on after he'd left the party and to be tuned in on the small-bore gossip about him. He seemed unperturbed. "You know, I've never been this town's favorite son," he said, then rattled off the 1960 election figures in which Hyannis voted for Nixon over Kennedy by 4,515 to 2,873. He knew the exact figures.

But one thing did irk him about that crowd, he confessed. It was the pally, name-dropping of public figures: "Styles" for Senator Styles Bridges of New Hampshire, and "Dick" for Senator Richard Russell of Georgia. "I've known him ever since I was a young congressman and I've never called him anything but *Senator* Russell," said the President with asperity.

Thus, in a few days of President-watching at Hyannis, JFK had been seen in all his fascinating, fetching, puzzling complexity. He had been the dare-devil golf cart driver, the candy-buyer, the newsprint-hog, the Uncle Pied Piper, the party-goer, the boatman, the exchanger of badinage and small talk, but still, ever the President, conscious of the dignity of his office and of that of U.S. Senators.

President Kennedy had been determined, on January 20, 1961, to be a vigorous, visible, do-something President. But there was the restless, roving spirit in him that pined for the salt air and sea of Hyannis. As had other Presidents before him, he learned he had to escape Washington. Still, ever jealous of his "image" as a strong President, he was nettled when his name became too much associated with Cape Cod. At the end of the summer, the Associated Press toted up the number of weekends he'd spent at Hyannis.

He did not care for such statistics and the memory of the newspaper story festered. At a luncheon, honoring publication of the John Adams papers, Kennedy was the chief speaker. Adams, he noted, spent whole summers at Quincy, Massachusetts, while Chief Executive, but, said Kennedy, "I suppose for one who has spent, in the words of the A.P., fourteen straight weekends at Hyannis Port, we should not be too critical. But it does indicate there was a different and more satisfactory pace in those times."

One striking thing about the Kennedys in Hyannis, as well as in Washington and in Palm Beach: they lived well. They were not stylish or ostentatious, but they exuded a kind of casualness that is far more expensive than it looks. There were always swarms of servants about, taking care of the nagging, homely chores that so complicate life for us lesser economic classes. There were helpers to tote the picnic lunches to the *Honey Fitz*, to keep an eye on the small fry, to hang out the laundry, to materialize at an elbow with a Coke, or Jackie's special summer drink, iced tea laced with apricot juice. There was "Sandy," introduced as the children's "physics" instructor, who turned out to be no nuclear expert but a muscular young man who taught the young Kennedys water-skiing and gymnastics. There was Muggsy to walk with Caroline, run an errand, fetch a car, or deliver an invitation. There were the nurses, the cooks, the maids, and the repair men.

But Hyannis, its patrician sheen well cloaked, was the place where the President lived his most vital self. Tretick's golf cart picture, in color, appeared on the cover of *Look* magazine January 2, 1962, and no picture ever taken of JFK so exudes the youth, the zest, the vitality, and the pure hunger for life that this one does.

He is squinting into the sun, the breeze brushing his thatch of hair. His broad grin is an excited one. He is clad in a blue polo shirt, sailor pants, and blue socks, and he is guiding the flying cart nonchalantly with one hand while the other arm embraces a nephew. In his lap, a niece is clutching the wheel, while a total of eight small-fry Kennedys look ahead to coming hazards with expressions of gleeful fear. The picture radiates danger, thrills, and fun with the Pied Piper. That was the way it was in Hyannis in the brief summer days of John Kennedy.

Trotting up the dock en route to the Honey Fitz, *and a day of sailing, the ebullient President is trailed not by a Secret Service man but by his old, "close" friend, K. LeMoyne Billings.*

Above: A smart clap of the hands by JFK was the signal that a rollercoaster ride was about to begin.

Right: Young Kennedys came streaking out of bushes, houses, away from the beach and the trampoline, to scramble aboard.

Whizzing by at PT-boat speed came a golf cart overflowing with junior Kennedys—were there 6, 8, 10?—but there was no mistaking the Kennedy at the wheel wearing comfortable, knockabout clothes. It was Himself.

The President zoomed that golf cart up, down and around the rolling compound hills, while the kids shrieked and their nannies quaked on the sidelines. Right: once he wheeled and came head-on at the photographer.

"Is that a fact," Uncle Jack said with fascination about the hot news imparted by David Kennedy, Maria Shriver, and Michael Kennedy.

The President
and his son

He was just a few months shy of three years old, an age when a child begins discovering that a father can be quite as interesting and necessary a human as a mother—and between the President and his son John, Jr., flourished an open mutual admiration society. He was the only son of the President, who had lost another, Patrick, in infancy only weeks before.

When this brown-eyed, kinetic buster, whose very build was so much like father's, burst into the Oval Office, the President brightened at the sight of him as he did for no Cabinet officer. "Hello, Sam," could be Daddy's greeting; this teasing would provoke the small boy to protest in a loud-decibel voice: "No No No, my name is *John*."

The special tie between father and son has long engrossed novelists and dramatists. There is something fiercely primitive and elemental about the relation; it is a deep and intricate emotion that touches on the human longing for the perpetuation of the self, the unconscious desire to continue the life stream through flesh and blood. No monument or honor can match the fulfillment a father feels when he beholds his son. He may adore a daughter, but with a son he feels he has been reborn, and from the moment of that rebirth, a father is filled with a tenacious, ancestral pride in what he hopes will become a better self.

All this could be seen in the eyes of John F. Kennedy when he glimpsed John, Jr. He doted on his daughter Caroline. In a way, he had "discovered" her when the campaigning was over and they had moved into the White House, for until then he had been a father much away from home. She had *carte blanche* to burst into his bedroom first thing in the morning to share an orange juice with him; he taught her little poems, and when she recited them without mistake he "took such pride" in her performance, his wife said, as he did "when the people he loved did things well." He listened to Caroline's made-up stories, and added imaginative embellishments of his own. Theirs was a tender, luminous bond.

But John, Jr., was a real male kin spirit. There was something special going between this father and his young son, a joyous, funny, mutually fascinated, male-to-male, even sensuous relationship. The President couldn't seem to resist grabbing for this small boy when he came within reach to tousle his hair, or give him a friendly pat on the fanny. "He never said so," said Mrs. Kennedy in the summer of 1964, talking about that painful subject, the loss of Patrick, the child they both wanted so much. "But I know he wanted another boy. John was such pure joy for him. He was the kind of man who should have had a brood of children . . . Most men don't care about children as much as women do—but he did—he felt the loss of the baby in the house as much as I did."

Behind the Kennedy New England reserve lay unexpected latent pools of gaiety, warmth, and fierce tribal affection. He was a man who kept his emotions in leash but they ran deep. He was not a man ashamed to kiss his father, or to weep when Patrick died, and to see him with his son was to see quite another Kennedy. In all the pictured glimpses of JFK, it is those with the children that even now so move the heart: there is a rapport there, a serious attention, so much naked intensity of feeling. If, as a special President, he was the essence of modernity, he was also a rare old-fashioned father.

To columnist Richard Wilson, who long before November 22 wrote that "President Kennedy in his public and family life has set the very highest standard of American conduct," Mrs. Kennedy sent one of her hand-penned notes of personal gratitude: "It is extraordinary to see these things written by someone who has never really seen him with his family . . . I am so glad you wrote it, not for other people to see, but for me. Now I will have it to show my children, later on, about their father."

Few pictures of the multipictured Kennedy captured this spirit so precisely and spontaneously as the candids, which by one of those odd quirks of publishing, appeared in *Look* magazine just four days before the Kennedy motorcade passed before the Texas School Book Depository Building in downtown Dallas.

In their grief, Americans wept afresh over these pictures. In Omaha, Nebraska, where the Midwest Governors' Conference was in stunned adjournment, Governor George Romney of Michigan stood transfixed, looking at the cover of John F. Kennedy and his son. He was a father, and there was a mist of understanding in his eyes. He shook his head, and said: "Now, through this terrible thing, these pictures are historic."

It was an "act of God" that they were taken, says Mrs. Kennedy, for they were not only a last closeup of the tender, prideful relation JFK had with his boy, but they almost didn't happen at all. The idea was born eighteen months before—and came off only, in truth, because the pictures were "sneaked" with Presidential help while Mrs. Kennedy was off cruising in the Greek islands. "Pierre and Jack," she says wryly, "were like two sneaky little boys letting you take those pictures while I was on vacation."

The President unwittingly sparked the idea himself, with an offhand remark. Tretick and I just happened to be talking to his secretary, Mrs. Lincoln, and wondering aloud whether her doting, nonrelative aunt relationship with Caroline could be photographed, when out from the Oval Office burst the restless JFK. We then and there asked him. "Well I don't know about Caroline," he mused, "*John's okay*, but not Caroline." He didn't spell out why, but perhaps Caroline nearing five, was of an age to be flustered by the publicity which so irked her mother, while John, then nearing a year and a half, wasn't?

His own phrase "John is okay," inspired in turn a Tretick letter, on June 26, 1962, the first of a half dozen such heart-rending appeals. "Dear Mr. President . . . Something you said last week when you were talking to Laura Bergquist and myself gave me an idea for a sensitive story with a lot of appeal. We were discussing Mrs. Kennedy's objections to photographs of Caroline, and Laura cited the picture of John, Jr., and Caroline playing in your office which the White House released. At that point you said 'John is okay.' The story I have in mind would be titled simply 'The President and His Son' and would be composed of pictures of only the two of you together, preferably on a weekend at the Cape. It could possibly be done in one shooting session, the earlier in the summer the better."

Back came the electric, incredible news, through Mrs. Lincoln, that the President had liked and approved the idea at once. Just why this seemed near miraculous was spelled out in an early New Frontier dispatch by UPI's Merriman Smith. "To say there is unhappiness among photographers covering the White House is necessitated because this is a family newspaper . . . There is a certain sameness about groups of men posed around Mr. Kennedy's office desk, but little John Kennedy crawling on the floor of his nursery or playing with his mother and sister—these are the pictures the public eats up."

Thus far Caroline had been the White House child star, overshadowing John. But who even knew what Junior looked like? Actually, early views of him as a baby had revealed he was no raving beauty—he looked like a "newly hatched robin," Mrs. Kennedy fondly recollects—and Stanley had nicknamed him Irving, a tag that stuck with the Press Corps.

Brief, tantalizing glimpses of fast-growing Irving had popped up off and on, greeting astronauts or peering over a White House balcony watching the helicopter depositing some new visitor-of-state on the lawn. There had been a news flurry, when some critics carped about his shaggy Prince Charles hair-do as somehow un-American. But he was still an unknown Kennedy, a mystery, of all unlikely things.

But eighteen cliffhanging months were to drag on, before, for various tangled reasons, the President—usually a quick decision-maker—finally gave the go-ahead. The intricate negotiating was conducted chiefly through Mrs. Lincoln, which sheds some light on the Kennedy Presidency and his press relations. Pierre Salinger officially handled newsmen, but if you wanted to slip a note to JFK, transmitting some precious idea, Mrs. Lincoln would hand it directly to Himself—only, of course, if her nearly infallible intuition told her the President would be interested. Pierre didn't mind. JFK was his own best press secretary, he once admitted.

Now Mrs. Lincoln, a homey, folksy, Nebraska-born lady then nearing fifty, at first might seem an odd Girl Friday for so jet-speed a President whose staffers ran, in the public mind, to Harvard eggheads and shrewd Boston Irish pols. But in her disarming, low-key way "Miz" Lincoln, whom Kennedy never never called Evelyn even after eleven years, set a cozy, *en famille* tone for the Presidential office. She answered the telephone as if she had all the time in the world, sprinkling her talk with "all righty." Her verdict on most of the world's VIP's who trekked past her desk was simply "real nice."

The President, a curious mixture of warm informality crossed with dynamo, liked relaxed people around him. But more important, Mrs. Lincoln was self-effacing devotion, discretion, and loyalty incarnate, qualities highly prized by New Frontiersmen for whom self-centeredness was a crime. She lived and breathed JFK. The depth of her loyalty was presumably spelled out once by Kennedy himself. He said that if he impulsively murdered someone, then buzzed for Mrs. Lincoln and asked her to file away the body, she would do so, no questions asked.

She also happened to be a great favorite of both Kennedy children. Caroline would dash in from the playground to plunk on her electric typewriter or filch a chocolate from the supply Mrs. Lincoln kept perennially handy for visitors. But it was John who was the new visitor to the West Wing, and it was Mrs. Lincoln who could fathom every last word of his fractured baby talk and watched with auntly pride his first tipsy attempts to walk.

She was also a great friend to have in court, not only because she was a sympathetic presence there in the seat of power, but she knew the nuances of the Presidential mood. When prospects looked most hopeless, she'd buoy us on with "He'll do it, I know the President will do it." That was another Kennedy characteristic: when he said yes, he meant yes, and when he said flat-out no, he meant no. When he rejected an idea instantly, for whatever reason, that was *it*, and no arguing or blandishment could budge him. Three times, for example, he vetoed a proposal to profile the "Flying White House," and how he worked aloft aboard *Air Force One*. He wanted no cameras poked into his private cabin; in his editorial judgment, as he told Kenny O'Donnell, *Air Force One* looked too much like a "rich man's plane."

He didn't want to look like an overprivileged President in the public prints.

Roundabout, came further word that JFK thought the "President and his Son" was one of the "best ideas" he'd heard in a long time. Still, one setback followed another, who knows even now exactly why? First, the Caroline crises intervened. Once, beseeched for an umpteenth time about John, Jr., JFK said hesitatingly that perhaps, well, the pictures might be taken in Palm Beach over the Christmas holidays—that again, was odd,

for it wasn't his usual crisp executive yes. And sure enough, in Palm Beach, Salinger merrily called out: "I've got bad news, the John, Jr. story is off."

One possible reason for Presidential hesitancy then, as we learned later, was that the youngster was going through a "difficult phase." Like many small boys, emerging from babyhood, he hadn't yet quite hit it off with Pop. That remarkable father-son rapport was to blossom a few months later when John, a late talker, began babbling a blue streak and sprouted into the all-boy personality who so intrigued his father.

Then at last came a break: a small news item announced that Mrs. Kennedy was going on a cruise through the Greek islands with her sister. Her husband, knowing how desperately she needed some respite after the loss of Patrick, urged her to go. There were to be some press jibes about the President's wife hobnobbing with the likes of Aristotle Onassis on a luxury yacht. JFK knew there would be static, he told his wife, but her welfare came first.

Perhaps Mrs. Kennedy had been the chief stumbling block all along, so we probed the White House again. "Call me a little later," said Mrs. Lincoln; "You mean Friday after 11 A.M.?" (the hour of Mrs. Kennedy's departure) asked Tretick. "Well, I didn't say that, but it might be a good. idea," was her diplomatic reply.

Voila, on October 7, came a blithe call from Salinger: if Tretick wasn't doing anything on the morrow, a Wednesday, how about coming to the White House to do a little story on John, Jr.? (What had impressed the President, he told his wife, had been Stanley's dogged, never-say-die persistence over eighteen months. He was no quitter, and that was another highly OK quality in the Kennedy book.)

Solo, at the working crack of Wednesday morning, Tretick had a conference with JFK who said candidly: "Now we'd better get this one out of the way pretty quick. Things get kind of sticky when Mrs. Kennedy is around."

His next brisk question: "Who's the writer on this story?" Now that was a stunner in itself, for how many Presidents would know that in the peculiar trade of photojournalism picture stories require *writers*?

"Laura," said Stanley. President: "Then where is she?"

Feebly, Tretick had to explain to the Chief Executive that at the moment the writer was meeting a deadline in New York. Besides, he didn't know whether the President would want an extraneous person hanging around his inner sanctum for hours, perhaps days.

That apparently struck Kennedy as preposterous, as it would any knowledgeable editor: His sound reasoning: "How is she going to get the *mood* of the boy?"

Then one more professional question by the editor-President: What should John do? Just what came natural, said Tretick; no posing of any kind except perhaps sitting still for a cover photograph. That suited JFK— for whom formal posing was a "let's-get-this-over-quick" ordeal—just fine.

"The *President Himself* says the story needs a writer," phoned a frantic Tretick. One possible stand-in was a political writer in the Washington Cowles Bureau, who had done a slew of articles on Kennedy and the New Frontier. But when Pierre Salinger erupted from the Oval Office, demanding "Where is Laura? How is she going to get the mood of the boy?" this proposal set off Gallic fireworks. "It's not *his* kind of story," exploded Pierre, and indeed it wasn't. The President, who had journalists pegged by specialties, was not accepting a political writer on an intimate family story.

All day Wednesday, before my hurried arrival, Tretick waited, camera at the ready, in the hall outside the Presidential office for John to appear. Nothing happened. By 6 P.M., suffering the acute depression non-happenings can inflict on a photographer, he packed his gear, ready to head for home. But no, Mrs. Lincoln urged, stay on, and her hunch, as always, was sound. For at 7:10 P.M., the witching hour when there was a lull even in the White House that made a fetish of a fourteen-hour working day, a Presidential voice called out: "Get Stanley in here."

And there in the Oval Office was a sight to gladden the eye and camera—ebullient, spirited John in pajamas and robe, careening about merrily and with innocent irreverence. It was his pre-bedtime visit with father. Both children usually were confined to East Wing living quarters, but with mother away, had special leeway to drop in on father in his working wing.

"How do you like him? Isn't he a charge?" was his father's immediate question. That seemed to be his overriding parental concern, those few days; were visitors as diverted and delighted by this terrific character as he was?

"What do you call your son, Mr. President," asked Tretick. "Why, John, of course," said JFK with some surprise. By now, he'd left off calling him John John, the nickname he'd given him to avoid the use of Johnny. The formal introduction was, "John, this is Mr. Tretick, a photographer from *Look* magazine." That couldn't have made much sense to a two-and-a-half-year-old, but both children were always properly introduced to any visitor. Caroline's response was a curtsy, John's a handshake, plus a cockeyed bow crossed with imitative curtsy.

It was the children's hour, but still Kennedy went back to rapid reading of the papers piled high on his desk, when John ducked out of sight, crawling under the Presidential desk. For John the space under the carved oaken timbers of that desk, made from the old British ship H.M.S. *Resolute*, was "my house." Suddenly a front panel swung open and out he tumbled through a "secret door," originally the discovery of Caroline. In a few

minutes as he crawled in and out, under the working President's feet, the kind of pictures happened you could never pose or dream up. That door was a marvelous stage prop for small-boy dramas, usually played with Dave Powers, special buddy of John. Junior would hide behind the secret door. Powers would knock, and ask: "Is the Bunny Rabbit in there?" Out would burst Junior, laughing his head off, while Powers duly registered shock, surprise, astonishment no matter how many times the game was played.

Even for a Kennedy, this boy was perpetual motion itself, and when he whizzed by the Presidential chair, JFK reached out to corral Junior. He pulled up his bathrobe and pajamas, to rub the skin just above John's behind, and once, midway through a mock spanking, paused to give him a paternal caress.

There was also a late hour off-the-record visitor, as in ambled Randolph Churchill, journalist son of Sir Winston. His repute as a convivial tippler is no secret, and when a Filipino waiter brought in a bottle of scotch, and ice, Kennedy grew a bit edgy. Although he wasn't drinking himself, he shied away, like any astute pol, from visual association with alcohol. "Just keep John away from the booze," advised Stanley.

"John, why don't you tell Mr. Churchill a secret?" the President suggested. That turned out to be another favorite sport, in which Junior would buzz buzz something unintelligible into an ear, preferably father's; the proper response was that invented by Dave Powers, who would clap his head as if he'd heard the most earth-shaking news of his life, and shout "Oh No! No! No! No! Not that!" Mr. Churchill, imitating, put on a superb performance.

At 7:50, visit over, JFK took his son by the hand, and as they walked down the dimly lit outside corridor toward the living quarters, said, "Let's go see grandaddy," for the Ambassador, recuperating from a severe stroke, was a house guest that night.

Washington, those October days, was at its loveliest; the White House was dappled in brilliant fall sunshine, and the gardeners worked overtime clearing the lawns of autumn leaves. No matter how many times I'd been in the quiet Oval Office, only yards away from the traffic tangle on Pennsylvania Avenue, that old paralysis hit me, on greeting JFK. For despite the familiar informality, the presence of young John, he was still the President. As the picture taking went on, and Kennedy went his rounds, he seemed more preoccupied, withdrawn, than before, with little time for banter and small talk, though he warmed instantly when told what John had been up to that day. What, he asked, first off, did *I* think of John? A "buster," I replied in truth, for though one doesn't warm automatically to small children, even though they are Presidential,

John was an instant beguiler. He was not gorgeous, with a chipped front tooth, but out of this bright, friendly, uninhibited, unspoiled boy ideas and words bubbled loud and fast.

He usually was bursting with vital news. "The sky is turning!" he cried one night. He had seen a searchlight sweeping the sky. He loved military salutes and ceremonials. "Where's the parade? Where's the parade?" he would ask his nurse, Maud Shaw, then look heartbroken when she explained that "Mr. Haile Selassie has gone back home and there won't be a parade today."

He had the natural inborn Kennedy confidence. Strangers didn't faze him one whit. Once on a shopping expedition in Georgetown with Miss Shaw, a crowd gathered about him. He promptly began to shake hands warmly all around, asking, "What's your name? My name is John Fitzgerald Kennedy, Junior." If told that he was a big man, he'd promptly agree, showing a bicep and stating confidently, "Yeah, and I've got big muscles, too."

He went on a blimp ride with Caroline's nursery school class, but his heart belonged to planes, choppers, and rockets. "We've lost him to the Air Force," despaired JFK's Army Aide Major General Ted Clifton. In the White House Fish Room, John learned how to dismantle a small model of the Gemini space capsule, which housed two toy-sized astronauts. He would take it apart, open the doors and remove the astronauts and their special seats, which were "beds" to him. When Dave Powers failed to put the nose cone back on properly, John had to show him how.

His daily schedule was that of Mr. Vigor. He pounded Mrs. Lincoln's electric typewriter, romped with such resident White House dogs as Clipper, Charlie, Pushinka, Wolfie, and Shannon, constantly re-read a tattered book, *The Little Lost Kitten,* tried on for size such military headgear as the gold-braided hat belonging to General Maxwell Taylor, Chairman of the Joint Chiefs of Staff.

He was also the official mansion dispenser of chewing gum, handing out sticks as lavishly as his father distributed PT-boat tie clasps. He meticulously dropped the gum wrappers in a wastebasket and always saved one stick for Caroline. His sister in turn made sure that he was tidy. Before they took off in a plane to greet their mother, returning from vacation, she combed his hair. "You have to look nice, John. We're going to see Mommy," she said.

If someone told him, "You're cute," he'd race about, shouting, "I'm cute, I'm cute!" At the zoo, his favorite inmates were the snakes, but he could also give a nifty imitation of a chimpanzee scratching himself. Waiting endlessly, impatiently, for his father's office door to open, he would sit drawing airplanes on a scratch pad that Mrs. Lincoln provided or pore

through his favorite reading matter, *Aviation Week*. (He is still a constant reader of that journal.)

That week Stanley Tretick's camera caught a kaleidoscopic, close-up view of the President as well as his son. Prime Minister Cyrille Adoula of the Congo, leaving JFK's sanctum, was introduced to John, and the boy promptly appropriated Adoula's small tribal stool gift as his own. Red Blaik, former West Point football coach, and Kenneth Royall, one-time Secretary of the Army, came in with Attorney General Kennedy to report on the Birmingham race crises. John raced to greet this favorite relative with cries of "Uncle Bobby, Uncle Bobby!"

Crises, big and small, battered. On Thursday, Russia's Andrei Gromyko was closeted with the President. That didn't sit at all well with Junior. Miss Shaw patiently explained that he couldn't barge into the office because Mr. Gromyko was there. "G'omyko! G'omyko! G'omyko!" John bellowed proudly, but inaccurately, in a voice that must have been heard on Pennsylvania Avenue. When Miss Shaw shushed him, he threatened experimentally. "I won't like you," he said, to which she replied firmly: "Then I won't like you back." That calmed him and he promptly plunked himself down on Mr. Adoula's gift stool to draw more airplane pictures. For all his high spirits, John was a well-behaved boy.

High level talks were going on in the Oval Office that week because the Russians had delayed two U.S. convoys for fifteen hours on the autobahn leading to West Berlin. Once, when the Presidential door opened, there was a wondrous tableau: JFK, looking his most steely, was deeply engrossed in talk with McGeorge Bundy, Secretary of State Dean Rusk, Ambassador Llewellyn Thompson, Kenny O'Donnell, and Salinger. Somehow into this preoccupied group had sneaked young John. He merrily crawled in and out of his secret door, trying to snag the attention of his father or any of these oblivious big interlopers.

In the boring waits for Daddy, John was into everything. He tried to filch a chocolate from Mrs. Lincoln's supply, he rummaged in the papers and he spied a picture of himself in the news, bidding good-bye to father at an airport. "Why do the pictures always show me crying?" he protested. Answer: "Because the President is going away in a helicopter." That made no sense to him. "I like helicopters," he retorted. (A few months earlier he had called them "heprecops.") Once he tore into the empty Cabinet Room, with its high octagonal mahogany table, to clamber over the chairs. There, he was cornered for an interview. Did he prefer blimps or helicopters? To this masterful question, he yelled Helicopters! Helicopters!

As he sat immersed in serious discussion, and drawing pictures of blimps and planes, Salinger suddenly materialized behind his back. Pierre was amused by the "interview" but John wanted no third party eavesdropping. With an executive flourish, he waved Salinger *out, out* of the room. That small anecdote, related to a President grappling with Birmingham, Berlin, and the Congo, brought a rare smile to JFK's face.

Three days now, JFK had suffered our presence, and it was time to get out. It seemed presumptuous, downright unpatriotic, to bring up so niggling a problem as posing for a cover, but he set it for Friday noon, just before lunch. On Presidential orders, one pre-arrangement for the sitting was made: John had his hair cut. Another ceremony had taken place late that morning in the Rose Garden, and the cameramen dawdled and fiddled interminably, packing up equipment. Would they *never* leave?

The lunch hour edged on, the President worked steadily at his desk, John was restless, until the coast was finally clear. Preoccupied, his mind obviously on other things, impatient to have this over with, the President and his son strolled out the tall French doors from the Oval Office, into the fall sunshine. There came another maddening interruption, as John helpfully dashed back to get me a stick of gum.

There were only seconds to work; JFK sat down on a bench to play "Secrets" with his boy, bent him over his knee, gave him a mock spanking; and then came a fresh complication, as limousines drove up and Defense Secretary McNamara and Maxwell Taylor hurried into the Presidential office, for more crises talk.

Late that day, torn between gall and humility, I again brought up a final problem. A good color shot was still needed for the cover. Searching wildly for an angle that might inveigle him into a second sitting, I asked the President if he'd seen a recent picture of the Nixon family in which Richard, Pat, and the two daughters stood like waxworks dummies, with glazed, uneasy smiles, gazing over the grim Berlin wall? One more session, and that could be bested for certain. JFK grinned. "No," he said, "was it really that bad?"

In light of John's passion for helicopters, what about a picture of their departure for a Camp David weekend? Kennedy paused for thought, then made a snap, surprise decision: we could come to Camp David with him on Saturday.

In the lead jet helicopter that whirled off before the one carrying the President we flew low over the Potomac whose banks were a blaze of scarlet and gold autumn foliage. At the landing pad at Camp David, there was an official welcoming party of John, Caroline, and an assortment of Kennedy dogs.

Now getting a wriggling, small boy to sit still for a portrait takes a bit of strategy. The day before Salinger had exhibited a new gadget someone had sent the White House. It was a life-sized toy parrot with a tape recorder buried inside. Why the devil hadn't we thought to borrow it to divert John?

When the Presidential chopper thrashed to a landing, and John

streaked like lightning to greet his father, the President deplaned miraculously toting that very parrot. He had even pre-recorded a message and the parrot said spookily in that flat, familiar JFK voice: "My name is Poll Parrot. Would you like to fly with me in my helicopter?" John was thunderstruck, but he replied with aplomb: "Hi, Poll Parrot. Would you like a stick of gum?" Then, he streaked off. Not even the usual JFK hand clap, at which both children ordinarily came running, could fetch him back.

"Well I guess you have enough now," said the President, impatient to be off. Not really, Mr. President, said Stanley, to my horror. Maybe he could try all over again on Monday, lunchtime? "OK, OK," said JFK, before speeding off in a limousine with the children.

Then a Secret Service man dashed up, just as we were boarding the helicopter for the return trip to Washington, to say "The President wants you to come to the house right away."

When we entered the spacious mountainside retreat, Kennedy said "I don't want to keep fooling around until Monday. Let's make the pictures *now*." He didn't want an obvious Camp David background, so he and Stanley went off to work, some distance from the house, on a stairway that led down the mountainside. John wriggled and squirmed, anxious like his father to be out of this ordeal and have it over and done with. My parting gift from John was an acorn.

Those three astonishing, nearly round-the-clock days were the last and most intimate glimpses I had of JFK. We gave him a set of the pictures for the family album, and I heard that he trotted all over the White House, showing them off. He vetoed the use of only one: John Junior sitting in the Presidential chair. Mrs. Kennedy said as she leafed through an album of the "President and His Son" that she could only think what fun these two male Kennedys would have had together.

JFK on the subject of his son: "How do you like him? Isn't he a charge?"

Above: It was a favorite game telling Father a special secret.

Below: John, official White House gum dispenser, talked over some Matter of State with the President.

Right: Two very hard-working John Fitzgerald Kennedys.

There was something special
going between the President and
his only son, a relation joyous,
mutually beguiled, even
"sensuous," as Mrs. Kennedy
said later. Looking at these
pictures, she could only think
what fun these two male
Kennedys could have had together.

The President seemed more withdrawn and preoccupied, those four October days in 1963; but he always brightened at the very sight of John Jr.

Only five weeks before Dallas all of these pictures of the President and his son were taken. After, it seemed to Mrs. Kennedy, an "act of God" that they were taken at all.

Left: When the Attorney General showed up with Earl "Red" Blaik, to report on the Birmingham crises, John streaked to this favorite uncle, shouting "Uncle Bobby! Uncle Bobby!"

Left: To get John Jr. to stand still, if only for minutes, was a problem. The President solved it by sitting on a bench in the Rose Garden and urging his son to play that sure-fire game, "Secrets."

Right: Then he turned John over his knee and gave him a mock paddling, followed up by an affectionate paternal caress.

Above: John clambered into his father's big Presidential chair, trying it out for size. With Mother away, he had special leeway to explore the "working" West Wing of the White House.

Opposite: Irrepressible John, after a long wait, positively danced across the room to greet Father. JFK had been closeted that day with Premier Cyrille Adoula of the Congo, escorted by Angier Biddle Duke, then Chief of Protocol.

Above: John is properly introduced to Col. Earl "Red" Blaik and the Prime Minister of Austria. The small tribal stool and table had been left as gifts by the Congo's Premier, and since they were just John's size, he appropriated them.

Above: For impatient John, it was a trial waiting for Daddy, busy in the Oval Office. When he protested, his nurse, Miss Maud Shaw, set about consoling him, while Mrs. Lincoln looked on, amused and sympathetic.

Right: Victory! John sneaked in, kicked off his shoes, and crawled into his "secret" house beneath father's desk, while the President and McGeorge Bundy, Llewellyn Thompson, Dean Rusk, Pierre Salinger, and Kenneth O'Donnell once again were saving the world. The crisis this time: Berlin.

The Presidential day had ground to a
halt when in ambled a late visitor, Randolph
Churchill, son of Sir Winston. JFK had
a sudden, bright suggestion for his son: "John,
why don't you tell Mr. Churchill a secret?"

John had been leafing through his favorite reading matter, Aviation Week, when his favorite grownup buddy Dave Powers found him in the Cabinet Room. "Tell me a secret," Powers urged. John buzzed in his ear and then Powers clapped his head and shouted, "Oh no! Heavens no! Not that!" That response, as always, broke Junior up.

At Presidential retreat, Camp David, Maryland, John and Caroline raced to meet Daddy, who brought a special present: a toy parrot with tape recorder inside. Parrot at first puzzled John by talking in father's flat Boston-cum-Harvard twang.

On a glorious October day, 1963, John F. Kennedy and his favorite boy sit for a portrait at Camp David, the Presidential retreat.

Jacqueline:
"Let's go out and
kiss the wind"

She was chic, shy, and wide-eyed, and looked fragile as fine porcelain. She was regal in bearing, yet she spoke with the lilting voice of a child. She could be whimsical, naive on the surface, yet there was a durable, unyielding firmness beneath. She was graceful, young, terribly feminine, fiercely independent, merry, moody, fey at times, artistic by bent, expensively educated—and a fascinating enigma to her public, and probably her husband. Said Mrs. Eleanor Roosevelt, quite another style of First Lady, after their first meeting: "There's a lot more to her than most people realize."

"She's a woman who has everything, including the President of the United States," remarked Letitia "Tish" Baldridge, her social secretary, soon after the Inauguration. At thirty-one, Mrs. Jacqueline Lee Bouvier Kennedy was as special and provocative a personality as her husband: she was not only one of the youngest and wealthiest First Ladies in American history, but perhaps the most talented, beautiful, and imaginative, and for some skeptical politicans, altogether a wildly improbable kind of wife for a winning Presidential candidate.

Some political experts acidly predicted during the years of the great Kennedy build-up that Jacqueline's classy good looks and remote public air might defeat the candidate by robbing him of the envious housewife vote. Or, if that calamity did not befall him, at least niggling criticism of his apolitical, nonorganization wife would dog his days in the White House.

She was, said critics, much too glossy and patrician an article to appeal to plain old Americans, and once in the White House would prove but a poor "decorative bird in a gilded cage." Her pursuits, riding to the hounds in Virginia hunt country, writing delicate poetry, questing for antiques, or reading French novels in French, were much too rarefied for the Corn Belt. Nervous Kennedy admirers urged that she become more of a do-gooder, à la Eleanor, or more of the plain hausfrau like Bess Truman.

But Jacqueline went her own sublime, private way. A year after the Inauguration she had become the most discussed and admired Presidential wife since Eleanor herself, although the why of the public feeling remained as elusive as she was. Gallup polls found the public liked her more for what she *was*, than what she *did*—her looks, her good taste, the genteel air, the fact that she was a proud, affectionate mother. Her knowledge of foreign languages, and genuine interest in the White House did us credit abroad. Dissenters carped about her "little girl's voice," once described as sounding "expensive;" and they objected to her early, frequent absences from the White House, a habit that led one Washington columnist to observe that any broadcaster could sign off at night by saying "Good night, Mrs. Kennedy, wherever you are."

Perhaps the public, in its growing love affair with this rarefied nonconformist, sensed that she was being herself, hewing to her own life style with a serene but stubborn independence of spirit. "She does what she bloody well pleases," said a friend—which didn't mean she was an anarchist by nature (although her mother had noted a streak of rebel in her as a child) but that she went her own way even as JFK himself did. "Can't you persuade Mrs. Kennedy to do it," I once asked the President about a project involving his wife, that he favored. He merely shrugged and rolled his eyes heavenward.

Self-contained, unpressured, she walked John, Jr., around the White House grounds in his buggy. She redecorated the old mansion in impeccable taste. ("Pre-Jackie," cracked a Potomac society columnist, "this place looked like a Statler Hotel, even the ash trays seemed straight out of an Army PX.") She plunged headlong off horses. She eschewed political hand-shaking for the arts. Once, instead of playing the charming hostess when Congressional wives came to tea, she went off to New York to attend a performance of the London Royal Ballet, and left her husband to entertain in her stead, which nettled many of the ladies. She declined to see Washington newsmen, then privately invited foreign writers to dinner. Still, never playing center stage, in her own behind-the-scenes way she worked tirelessly at being the First Lady, and managed to raise two charming, unspoiled young children in the bargain. Soon JFK, ever a man to admire competence, was confessing with some surprise that he hadn't realized his wife had so much "executive ability." She was so impressively organized, said an awed member of her staff, she actually had the White House Christmas card list prepared by June.

The look of fragility was deceiving. In truth, she was a strong, big-boned beauty as fond of the outdoors as her husband—and as adept at sports. Her eyes were set a bit too wide apart for classic beauty, but seemed to be constantly alight—though when displeased she could look every whit as frosty and distant as her husband. In the country, she'd wear her dark hair casually—the "wind-blown look" JFK liked best—but often publicly in bouffant styles promptly copy-catted round the world. Women who at first complained that they were tired of reading about Jackie's clothes, her children, her galas, came in time to appreciate her taste, the working of her mind, her character, her serenity. "She changed the White House from a plastic to a crystal bowl," said Letitia Baldridge. "Leaving the glitter and glamour aside, the outstanding thing about her tenure of office was her impression on American girls—the young could identify with her and were influenced by her dignity, bearing, posture, quietness of voice, thoughtfulness, and warmth."

Men were apt to find her very distinct femininity most provocative. "My only trouble," once said writer Stewart Alsop lightly, "is that I'm in love with Jackie Kennedy." Regal in bearing and slightly "stiff with strangers,"

she could be smashingly informal in private and display a wicked but non-wounding wit. One diplomat could not take his eyes off her during their first meeting one evening. "She radiates," he said, somewhat overcome, "she sparks." Where her husband was the rationalist, she was intuitive, with strong likes and dislikes—and she could sum up a personality, newly met, with a few, colorful, well-chosen words. Of a young lady who forever seemed to be working for, or basking in, the limelight of the famous, her judgment was: "She's a nice girl, but sort of a pilot-fish, don't you think?" e.g. the kind of little fish that forever swims in the shadow of a big fish.

"Just when you think you understand her, you're in trouble," once said Dave Powers. Some of her mannerisms were at variance with the queenly presence. She sometimes seemed to look at the world with the wide-eyed wonderment of actress Marilyn Monroe, and her soft, low voice had a breathless Monroe edge to it. When she said "Oh yeah," she meant it not as a sarcastic challenge but wonderingly about some exciting event; when she said "How dreary!" it meant how appallingly dull. Many of the mundane chores of this workaday world were "dreary" to Jackie, and the princess in her recoiled from them.

If John F. Kennedy was politically trained for the White House since young manhood, Jacqueline was no less socially schooled to accompany him. Even though her mother was divorced when Jackie was a young girl and she lived in two households, both milieus gave her the gentled, sheltered early life of American Old Guard wealth-with-servants which in turn gave her the golden leisure for pursuing the Rare and the Beautiful. The cocooned security of those early years accounted, perhaps, for her serenity and independence of mind, and also that slight air of unreality.

She was born in Southampton, most fashionable of the Long Island Hamptons, July 28, 1929, daughter of Janet Lee and John Vernon Bouvier III. Her mother was a great American beauty of an affluent, and very social, New York family. Her father was a well-to-do stockbroker, of a French Catholic family that could trace its ancestral line to some twenty-four Bouviers who crossed the Atlantic to fight in the American Revolution. Jack Bouvier, in addition to being a Wall Streeter, was a cavalier and dashing figure nicknamed the "Black Orchid," and "Black Jack" because of his perpetual Arab-like tan. He was, says *New York Times* columnist Arthur Krock, an old family friend, "one of the most famously attractive men who ever lived, a great athlete, prom trotter and fusser," the last a word of 1920's vintage denoting a man with an electric effect on women. Jackie adored him.

Significantly, the two key men in her life were devastatingly attractive men, and in a way she was parted from them both, her father through divorce, her husband, soon after her marriage, by politics. When Jack Kennedy met his prospective father-in-law, they struck it off at once, talking politics, sports, and girls, while Jackie sat on the sidelines and listened.

160

Her girlhood in New York and Southampton, L.I., where the Bouviers summered, was a proper one. She learned to ride not long after she walked, and became a prize-winner at Hampton horse shows. She read voluminously and at an early age, when she much resembled her daughter Caroline, she began writing verses. She went to the right private schools, Miss Yates's and Miss Chapin's in New York, and with the proper white gloves, to dancing lessons at the Colony Club. Her younger sister Lee, to whom she has always been close, was the more placid of the two, Jackie the imaginative one with a quick-bubbling temper. Other girls, recalls her mother, worried "ten times more about clothes" than Jackie, who even as a youngster always looked "marvelously put together," while sister Lee seemed "blown out of a hurricane."

In 1942, when their mother was remarried to Hugh D. Auchincloss, a Washington, D.C., broker and bluff country squire, both girls went to live in his gracious mansion, Merrywood, which nestled in the Virginia woods on a ridge overlooking the Potomac River. They summered at the Auchincloss estate Hammersmith Farm at fashionable Newport, Rhode Island. Jacqueline loved both Merrywood and Hammersmith, and when away would write nostalgic letters about her sentiment for the homes.

The special milieu that shaped her was described by playwright-author Gore Vidal, a relative by marriage since his mother Nina Vidal had been married earlier to Hugh Auchincloss. Gore Vidal too had lived at Merrywood.

"It was a golden, peaceful life," he recalls, "a bit Henry Jamesian. . . . A world of deliberate quietude removed from twentieth-century tensions. The depression, the war in Spain impinged very little on us, though you heard plenty of anti-New Deal opinion. Actually eighteenth-century English politics seemed more real since a family step-uncle, Wilmarth Lewis, was a famous Horace Walpole scholar. It was a life that gave total security, but not much preparation for the real world which burst on us as a great adventure and big discovery. Most of us broke away. Jackie surely rejected the Great Lady tradition of her mother. But we all in one way or another tried to recreate Merrywood's heavenly ambiance in our own households."

In Washington, Jacqueline attended Holton-Arms, a private school, where she learned Spanish in addition to the French that she had learned as a small girl. Then she went off to still another correct school, Miss Porter's School in Farmington, Conn., where she specialized in literature, English, and art. An added inducement was the fact that she could keep her own horse in the school's stables. Also, at Miss Porter's, she spent many gay weekends with her father who came calling to take Jackie and her friends out to dinner.

When she graduated, her life's ambition was noted as: "*Not* to be a housewife," and she was "most known for" her wit.

It was the kind of background that requires little more of a girl, especially a very pretty one, than to be decorative, dabble a bit in the arts, and marry well. A girl with talent isn't expected to pursue it terribly seriously, or if she's well endowed with brains, doesn't flaunt that fact.

She went on to attend Vassar College for two years. (Much later, noting the ample quota of Harvard men and Vassar graduates on the White House staff, an observer remarked that the "coat of arms for this administration should be a daisy chain on a field of crimson.")

She did very well, scholastically, at Vassar, but what really shaped her thinking, and personality, was the year of study at the Sorbonne. "Tish" Baldridge was then performing social secretary duties for Mrs. David Bruce, wife of the U.S. Ambassador to France, and she recalls Jackie as a girl who immersed herself in French literature, lived with a French family, and traveled all over the Continent whenever she could. She had made her first Grand Tour after her freshman year at Vassar, and wrote an illustrated log of the journey for her Auchincloss step-brothers and sisters. Gifts that took thought and doing were typical of her daughter, says her mother, recollecting that when at eighteen Jackie came back from the first great European adventure, she brought a rosary blessed by the Pope for the pious maid, and an English racing form for the horse-playing butler.

But that independent year in France spoiled her for returning to Vassar where she would have had to "live like a little girl again," and so instead she took courses at George Washington University, including some training in journalism.

That led to her lone paying job, as inquiring photographer for the now defunct Washington *Times-Herald*, obtained largely through the intervention of Arthur Krock, who managed to enter the lives of both Jacqueline and JFK at strategic times. Her pay: $42.50 a week, raised eventually to $56.75.

Now popping up before strangers-on-the-street with a camera and a question was no job for a shrinking violet. Several times weekly she buttonholed stray Washington citizens, and although the headlines were black with news of McCarthyism and the Korean War, her own made-up questions ducked such explosive issues and ran to the erudite and/or whimsical: e.g. "How do you feel about George Bernard Shaw's statement that youth is too good to be wasted on young people?" Or: "In George Bernard Shaw's *Doctor's Dilemma* a doctor must choose between saving the life of a great artist who is a scoundrel or a commonplace honest family man. Which would you save?" On this question, three citizens opted for the artist, but a physician slid away from the dilemma by answering: "I'd save whichever one would respond best to medical treatment." Another Jackie question was: "What were you thinking of when I stopped you?" Replied a flower vendor:

"I thought you were going to buy some flowers." Said a typist: "I was thinking about my boy friend. We quarreled last week and lately the phone hasn't been ringing like it should. Bernie honey, are you reading this?" Replied a liquor store owner: "I was thinking of how to pull off a perfect crime. They'll lock me up when they read this."

All that was harmless newspaper fluff, but the column was well read in the capital. Frequently, since Washington is a city drenched in politics, Jacqueline carried her camera and questions to government office buildings and to Capitol Hill. One day, two ambitious young politicians were among those answering the question, "What's it like observing the Senate pages at close range?" They were the new Vice President, Richard M. Nixon, and the boyish Senator from Massachusetts, John F. Kennedy. Nixon and Kennedy saw alike on this weighty problem and responded in character to it. Said Nixon: "I would predict that some future statesman will come from the ranks of the page corps." Said Kennedy: "I've often thought that the country might be better off if we Senators and the pages traded jobs."

Occasionally, Jacqueline was unleashed from the column to do feature stories. One of them was a color piece on President Eisenhower's first Inauguration. With a deft eye for detail about First Ladies, Jackie noted that "Ike planted a kiss on Mamie's cheek right after the oath." (When President Kennedy failed to do likewise to his wife, the White House received a number of protests.) Jacqueline also recorded at Ike's Inauguration that "Mamie's lively laughter could be heard far back in the crowd . . . Mrs. Truman sat stolidly with her gaze glued to the blimp overhead."

As another Inaugural feature, she did an offbeat interview with the president of the National Seating Company, who rented folding chairs for the stands, neatly profiling him as "a man who almost hates to see anyone stand up. I found him sitting in front of the White House on a $3 kitchen chair rented by him at $5 an hour."

Later in 1953 she traveled to London on her own funds and reported the Coronation of Queen Elizabeth for the *Times-Herald*. She filed lively copy, including an amusing account of a "Mesta Fiesta," a dinner ball thrown at Londonderry House by hostess Perle Mesta. "Lauren Bacall was the belle of the ball," chattered Jackie as she dropped names and fashion notes left and right. "She had a swooping waltz with General Bradley, then a series of romantic fox trots with the Marquess of Milford Haven. She wore a tight white-lace dress and her long scarlet finger nails rested lightly on his highly burnished epaulettes. Bogie, wearing a plain old white tie and tails outfit, cut in on her." She sent along a cartoon of this tableau showing a glowering, crew-cutted Humphrey Bogart waiting to cut in on the suave, glittering Marquess.

A fan cabled her from Washington, approving the coverage: ARTICLES

EXCELLENT BUT YOU ARE MISSED. When her plane landed in the United States, the fan was at the airport to welcome her home. He was Jack Kennedy.

Their romance had been slowly gathering steam for two years. They had met in the summer of 1951 at the narrow Georgetown house of Charles and Martha Bartlett. Earlier Jackie had been squired about several times by Bartlett, a close friend of Jack Kennedy since their meeting at Palm Beach right after World War II. Bartlett, a machine-gun conversationalist with Kennedy-like mannerisms, was Washington correspondent for the *Chattanooga Times*. With an eye to making a match between two handsome, eligible people, the Bartletts invited Jacqueline Bouvier and John Kennedy to a dinner party for eight. As Jackie now recalls the meeting, she decided at once that Kennedy was a man whom she'd enjoy seeing a great deal. The Senator's reaction, while favorable, was more fluid. He was having a great time as a bachelor and besides, he was beginning to haunt the state of Massachusetts on weekends preparatory to a race for Henry Cabot Lodge's Senate seat.

Kennedy took Miss Bouvier dancing several times and now and then phoned her from Massachusetts, but their contacts were too occasional to be labeled a courtship. After Kennedy's election to the Senate in the fall of 1952, however, their dating took on more serious flavor. They went off to the movies with Robert and Ethel Kennedy or by themselves, they dropped in on the Bartletts, they drove to Merrywood with Kennedy piloting his convertible in his usual PT-boat style. One thing struck Jacqueline during the courtship that ranged geographically from Palm Beach to Cape Cod. Unlike the bolder Ivy League products who had wooed her, never once did this suitor propose they go off for a night or a weekend. From the beginning, Jacqueline recalls, "You know, Jack was something special, and I know he saw something special in me, too. I remember my mother used to bring around all these beaus for me but he was different."

That airport welcome led to a proposal of marriage. The bachelor Senator had brought up the subject earlier, but said he wanted to wait. But when he did decide to marry, he told Jackie, she'd be the girl. "Well," she replied, "how big of you!"

It was quite a wedding. Held at Hammersmith Farm in Newport, it brought together the worlds of politics, war veterans, and East Coast society. The extravaganza went on for several days; there was a bridal dinner, two bachelor dinners, one for politicians in Boston and another for the wedding party at Newport, receptions, lunches, cocktail parties, and a giant route for the twenty-six bridesmaids and ushers at the Kennedy compound at the Cape. The bridesmaids included match-making Martha Bartlett, new sisters-in-law Ethel Kennedy and Jean Smith; Kennedy's ushers included old friends Bartlett, Congressman Torbert MacDonald, his Harvard roommate, Senator

George Smathers of Florida, Lem Billings and PT-boat buddy Paul C. (Red) Fay, Jr., later to become Under Secretary of the Navy. At the bachelor dinner, Kennedy's friends were so carried away they twice hurled expensive wine glasses into the fireplace in toasts to the bride. When Hugh Auchincloss saw another toast coming up for his step-daughter, he hastily summoned a waiter and gave orders that a less costly brand of glassware be substituted. Jackie's father, the durable, dashing "Black Orchid," particularly enjoyed the fireplace explosions, no doubt on the sound ground that it was the step-father of the bride, not the father, who would have to replenish the wine glass stock.

One night, just before the ceremony that moved society reporters to new rapturous adjectives, Kennedy drew aside one of his World War II buddies and asked him what he thought of Jacqueline. Smashingly beautiful, granted the friend, but *what about that voice?* Kennedy grinned: "You'll get used to it."

The wedding, September 12, 1953, drew some 800 distinguished guests to St. Mary's Church in Newport, a congratulatory message from the Pope, and some 3,000 curious spectators who broke through the police cordon and almost trampled the bride. Although Jacqueline's mother was an Episcopalian, her father was a Roman Catholic and Jackie had been reared in that faith. Archbishop, later Cardinal, Cushing of Boston, officiated at the nuptial Mass. The bride was duly described as "radiant" wearing a lace veil in which her grandmother had been married. The bridegroom, of course, was the catch of the year.

The Senator was indeed one of America's most eligible bachelors, lean, lithe, handsome, a millionaire, and fortune's darling, but there was enough of the Irish in him to realize that, in some ways, his bride outclassed him. A Washington society reporter, who reported the event, sniffed privately that, after all, "Jack" was marrying above his social station. The Bouviers were not only old guard, Republican, old money society, but they had that prestigious ancestral line dating back to the Revolution. JFK, for all his natural class, was still the grandson of Irish immigrants. His grandfather "Honey Fitz" Fitzgerald had been the merry mayor of Boston who sang "Sweet Adeline" on table tops in Irish bars at campaign time. Father Joe Kennedy may have been Ambassador to Great Britain, but still the Kennedys by the standards of society studbooks were *nouveau-riche* and late comers. French Catholics, furthermore, were held to be more chic than the Irish variety.

In tandem, they seemed the golden couple-with-everything, this bridegroom of thirty-six and his bride of twenty-four, and they went off to honeymoon at Mexico's Acapulco, one of the world's more spectacular resorts where the hills rise sheer from the sun-laved Pacific harbor. They lived in a pink cliff-side house that Jackie had visited earlier, and JFK celebrated the new marriage by boating a sailfish which, mounted, later adorned both his Senate office and the Fish Room at the White House.

Jacqueline came home to Washington and two demanding new roles, that of the wife of a U.S. Senator, and that of a Kennedy wife. Both were difficult, but of the two, finding her niche in the boisterous, competitive, close-knit Kennedy family required the more ingenuity and skill. "I wasn't very interested in politics before I married Jack," she said, "but I'm learning by osmosis." She attended a few meetings of the Senate wives, where she was regarded as the sweet little bride, and soon dropped out. She preferred to be less of the joining, organization politico's wife, but privately was of great help to her husband on occasion with homework. As a sample, when he was boning up on the Indo-China war, which later was to plague him as President, she translated a mound of books and documents from the French for him. She attended Senate hearings, in which her husband was a participant, but stayed aloof from the elephantine Washington cocktail circuit. Her forte was the small dinner party, where she steered conversation into channels that might be expected in the home of writers or university intellectuals. Occasionally, when she did hostess a political do for her husband, she appeared slightly out of place. At one crush, in their rented Georgetown house, she looked bewildered, even frightened, by the din and clatter of jokes and political yarns swapped by happy Democrats from Massachusetts.

Adapting to the swarm of Kennedy in-laws, nephews, and nieces, took patience and decisiveness. She has been quoted as saying she fell in love instantly with the family, but her actions indicate the love was tempered by some irritation, and even stubborn revolt. Married at a relatively sheltered, unformed twenty-four, she was, says a friend, at first "snowed" by the Kennedy tribe that was apt to steam-roller outsiders or make them over in the Kennedy image. But she managed to remain stunningly unlike them. Their togetherness simply wasn't her cup of tea. At Hyannis, where the family motto was "My house is your house," at the end of a day of sizzling outdoor fun and games, one of the sisters cried: "Now we're all going over to the big house." "*You're* going over to Joe's," replied Jacqueline firmly. "*We're* having guests for dinner." Other Kennedys learned not to drop in on the John F. Kennedys without previous invitation. When she injured her heel playing touch football, *de rigeur* sport for Kennedy males and females alike, she retired permanently from the game. In her Georgetown house, she presided one night over a candlelit dinner: brother-in-law Teddy was newly back from revolution-torn Algeria, and the sheer noise of the talk grew deafening. "Good lord," she said with detached amusement, "Did you ever hear such a racket?"

When the self-improving clan took up speed-reading lessons, however, she bested them all: she was excused after the first lesson, as already speedy

166

enough, though JFK was not. "I was only halfway down the test page when she'd finished," recalls Jean Kennedy Smith, gentlest of the sisters and closest to Jackie.

It couldn't always have been easy to be married to an electric, ambitious man forever away from home on the campaign trail. "Public life burst on her when she wasn't prepared for it," said a Senator's wife. "Young, popular, pretty as a valentine, in need of incense, she promptly lost her husband to politics. He was an established politico, moreover, and for a long time she floundered, vaguely discontent, not knowing what her role was." Their residences showed an unsettled mood in their early years of married life. They lived briefly at Merrywood, then in a rented Georgetown house, and then in the country house, Hickory Hill, in McLean, Virginia, once owned by Supreme Court Justice Robert Jackson, and purchased by Joe Kennedy. It was too isolated for a childless couple, and held too many unhappy memories, after Jacqueline lost a child through miscarriage. Even the decor, said a close friend, was a mistake—"too phoney Italianate; the dining room walls were so bright pink they looked like an elaborate strawberry dessert." So they swapped the house with Bobby Kennedy for his Georgetown house—and not until Caroline's arrival did they purchase a home of their own, again in Georgetown.

The pre-Caroline years—there were four of them—had their trials for Jacqueline. She often seemed more ornamental than essential in her husband's life. He was a man's man, essentially, who with the years grew ever more patriarchal like his father. His world was politics, sports, ideas, events. The subtleties of the female psyche and mystique did not seem to intrigue him much, even though he had a healthy eye for pretty women. His relationship to his outgoing, somewhat tomboy sisters, was affectionate, bantering, rough-house. "Jackie never bombards him with questions, like we do," said sister-in-law Jean Smith. "She approaches him in a leisurely way, knowing that he'll talk about things when he's ready." Any unusual human, male or female, piqued JFK's interest, but he did not seem to me to take women as such very seriously. In the New Frontier inner circles, for example, there were no token appointments of VIP females; FDR had Francis Perkins in his cabinet and Eisenhower had Oveta Culp Hobby, but Kennedy dealt with no woman as an equal working partner.

Even their 1952 courtship had been a sporadic thing, savored like cocktail *hors d'oeuvres* in the flurry of his first race for the Senate. Then came his Vice-Presidential bid of 1956, and after that hardly a week went by when JFK wasn't flying about the country to address Democratic rallies. At times, he seemed thoughtless of her. When she lost a premature baby in 1956, he was vacationing in Europe, after the hullabaloo of the Democratic convention. After the 1960 election, he flew off to Palm Beach to plan his new administration, while she remained behind in Washington alone, heavy with unborn John, Jr., in the Georgetown house. The boy arrived prematurely, while the President-elect was still in Palm Beach, and Jackie rode alone in the ambulance to the hospital. Her one concern voiced to the doctor was "Can you save the baby?" At the Inaugural ceremony, when JFK didn't kiss his wife after taking the Presidential oath, wives fretted. On receiving some 400 letters asking why the kinetic new President seemed so often to walk ahead of his wife, Pierre Salinger brought this to Kennedy's notice. His amused quip: "Tell Jackie she'll just have to walk faster."

There were the strains of sickness and death, too, in this marriage. Of the four children she bore with difficulty, she lost two, and once nearly lost her own life as well. Then soon after her marriage she had to weather the near-fatal spinal operation on her husband. He had undergone one spinal disc operation in 1944, after the torpedoing of his PT boat, but in 1954 severe back pains returned. He took to crutches, lost weight, and began to look emaciated. The pain was so intense, he resorted to surgery rather than endure it longer. An operation in New York's Hospital for Special Surgery proved a failure and was complicated by his adrenal gland deficiency. The wound became infected, and for a time, the family thought he might die. He rallied at Palm Beach, underwent a second successful operation, and finally returned to the Senate floor in the early summer of 1955 after an absence of eight months.

Jacqueline, showing the steel the public glimpsed in her after the assassination, was a tireless attendant on her husband during this black period in their lives when it was uncertain that he would ever walk again. After the first operation, as he was mending, she brought him fresh daily surprises, from balloons he could shoot with a popgun from his hospital bed to glamorous Grace Kelly herself. She withstood these trials with such fortitude and stoicism that she won the admiration of her tough old father-in-law. "She's got what it takes," said the Ambassador, and thereafter he and this daughter-in-law, unlike as two human beings could be, became devoted friends.

On one wedding anniversary, she splashed out one of her whimsical, personally revealing water colors, as a gift for her husband, titled "How the Kennedys Spend Wedding Anniversaries." It was done gaily, but there was a certain poignancy about the theme. In Scene One, JFK lay flat on his back in a hospital bed, with long and doleful face. In Scene Two, she was the melancholic patient, he the bedside comforter.

The theme of so many of her paintings were inside family jokes. She sketched a whole series to illustrate a light article that her husband drafted for a magazine (unpublished), spoofing his labors during the 1956 Stevenson-Eisenhower campaign. One showed JFK, politico on the road, doing the homely chore of washing out his socks in a hotel bathroom. One Christmas she dashed off another lighthearted drawing for her sister-in-law Ethel Kennedy, energetic mother of an ever-growing brood of children and mistress of a household chronically plagued by servant problems. In the funny, affectionate vignette, Ethel suns by the pool, dictating matters of state to a secretary. Three sons gallop madly across the lawn on horseback, trying to lasso the governess. A newly hired maid trudges up one front driveway, while a departing maid leaves via another.

Her female intimates, apart from her sister the Princess, surprisingly tended both in Georgetown and the White House to hard-working young mothers and the wives of newsmen, with whom she felt she had a "great deal in common." One such was blonde, bright Tony Bradlee, a fellow Vassarite and a Boston Pinchot, wife of *Newsweek* Washington Correspondent Ben Bradlee. The Bradlees lived a few doors down the street from the Kennedys' Georgetown residence, and Jackie spent neighborly hours in the Bradlee kitchen while JFK was out speech-making on the road. "When she invited my children for lunch," said an awed Tony, "she invited all *four* of them."

Her early wifely influence on JFK included sprucing up his attire as well as his diet. As a Congressman, he had been known to show up on the House floor in tennis shoes and odd sports coats. She bought him shirts secretly, a dozen at a time, because of his habit of changing shirts three times daily. Under her tutelage, the Senator became quite a sartorial expert, given conservatively to two-button suits, *un*buttoned down shirts, and sedate ties. He was ever an *aficionado* of good shoes, contending the best were dark brown cordovan, which should be polished alternately with ox blood and black polish, and he frequently chided friends whose shoes tended toward the too red or yellow.

She also upgraded his diet, which had run heavily to fish chowder, hot dogs, ice cream, and milk shakes. He had a passion for chowder, brought to him daily for lunch in his Senate office by Muggsy O'Leary, but at home Jacqueline served him more exotic fare, like mangoes for dessert and *oeufs en gelée* as an appetizer. As a hostess, Jackie was no "cruise director," said a Senator's wife who was present at her first dinner party. She pulled such gaffs as serving soup with teaspoons, which didn't ruffle Jackie though it disturbed her mother, who also called her daughter's attention to what seemed to be a broken record on the phonograph. It was Fred Astaire tap dancing.

With the birth of Caroline in November, 1957, she was really "in" with the prolific Kennedy clan, and well settled in her marriage after the years of "vague discontent." JFK doted on his daughter. "From the time we had Caroline," his wife said, "Jack has been interested in all his friends' children. She has made him so much happier."

But he was also stepping up his travels even as Caroline grew, for he was now shooting for the biggest prize in world politics, the American Presidency. He flew everywhere, in response to speaking invitations, and by 1959, his office and home were aclutter with meetings as he began the hard, time-consuming job of gathering Kennedy-pledged delegates to the 1960 nominating convention. "I was always coming down to breakfast in my wrapper with Caroline," said Jackie later, "and there would be a couple of strange governors or labor leaders I'd never seen before, smoking cigars and eating scrambled eggs."

The Presidential campaign year was another testing time for Jacqueline. She was pregnant again, this time with John, Jr., even though some people didn't believe it. Some snide observers contended that the reported pregnancy was a blind to cover the Kennedy managers' unwillingness to expose such a polished article as Jackie to campaign crowds accustomed to more plebeian fare in candidates' wives. This theory actually got into print in Dorothy Kilgallen's column. "Do you think I should stuff a pillow under my dress to convince her?" impishly asked Jackie.

At first, she hadn't felt vitally "needed" on the campaign, but then when she saw evidence that her presence helped, she did what she could, pregnant as she was. After one TV appearance, a staffer said, "I was as proud as if my own child had done well, and the mail did begin to change in Jackie's favor, as against the early letters which tended to run, 'I'm an old woman of eighty and won't you please change your hair style.' When she was surrounded in depth by 1,000 women, it was hard on her, but in intimate appearances, on TV, or in small groups, she was marvelous." Jackie held listening parties, during the TV debates, and hundreds of ladies the country over followed her example.

During the Presidential primaries, she had accompanied her husband on many of his trips, shaking hands in snowy Wisconsin at factory entrances at 6:30 A.M. It wasn't always easy for her. In the early days of stumping with JFK, she would sometimes stand wistfully on the fringes of a politico do, looking ravishing but a bit forlorn. She could have been "naked as a jaybird," a friend observed, and still drawn little attention from the pols and her husband, absorbed in the mechanics of vote-getting. But she learned. Once, campaigning in a French-speaking section of New Hampshire, she evoked cheers by saying *"Moi aussi je suis d'origine française."* (I too am of French descent). Another time, seated six places away from JFK at a political lunch, she made the graceful sally: "This is the closest I've come to lunching with my husband in four months." Once, arriving in advance of her perennially tardy husband at a New York rally of 5,000 Reform Democrats, still madly for Adlai and a hard crowd for any Kennedy to please, she peeped out at the audience and panicked, saying, "I can't go on." Then mustering courage she sailed onstage, and said: "This is the first time in history I've arrived ahead of my husband." That light quip paved the way for her husband's opening remark: "I know there's somebody you'd rather see more [namely Stevenson], but I'm afraid I'm all you've got."

That West Virginia primary changed some ideas of the wise ones, who had thought that Jackie might prove a liability in the campaign. Muriel Humphrey, wife of Hubert, had been the very model of a hard-working political spouse. She was at her husband's side day and night, homey, folksy, handing out favorite recipes to housewives who might have been her neighbors in the old depression days in the upper Midwest. After an emergency call from the Kennedy staff, Jacqueline blew in, chic and pregnant, like a Cinderella from another world. The country people, whose daily lot was misery and impoverishment, far from being alienated were captivated by this emissary from the remote world of Culture, Affluence, and Style. Or as a surprised politico put it, they were "wowed by this classy tomato," who didn't flaunt her good fortune. At a local bake sale, she captured a number of housewives' votes by sampling every last cake on the counter.

If conditions in West Virginia were an eye-opener to Kennedy, they were a shock to Jacqueline. It was an America, she confessed, she had never seen before, and she commented with revealing naiveté: "I've never had much of a social conscience, but now I do. I know Jack intends to do something about all this." She was never to become a battler for social causes; she hadn't been a girl to picket or march in militant rebellion and as First Lady she never gave firm opinions about civil rights or the banning of the bomb. "I get all my political views from my husband," she once said, "not because I can't make up my mind on my own, but because he would not be where he is unless he was one of the most able men in his party. So I think he's right."

She was politically savvy enough to rejoice when Dr. Benjamin Spock, the widely read author and pediatrician, came out foursquare for JFK, knowing how influential he was with millions of young mothers. From brother-in-law Robert, campaign mastermind and hard nose "pol," came one assessment of what she'd done for the Kennedy fortunes: "We came out of that Los Angeles convention looking like a hard, tough family juggernaut. But in her few gentle, low-key TV appearances, Jackie softened that image and put the spotlight back where it belonged, on Jack and his family." Bobby spoke admiringly of her "guts," too. Despite doctor's warnings, when many months pregnant, she insisted on joining her husband's New York ticker-tape parade. It exhausted her, it was dangerous for her health, but she was glad she did it. "If he lost," she said, "I'd never forgive myself for not being there to help."

She'd had her reservations, when her husband set his sights on the Presidency. "It isn't the right time of life for us," she rued. "We should be enjoying our family, traveling, having fun."

But though she went along as the dutiful wife of the candidate, she never gave up a square inch of her individuality. What other wife of a Presidential aspirant could be found curled up on a campaign plane, reading Jack Kerouac's novel *Dharma Bums?* Or when asked her opinion on the best site for the Democratic national convention, would suggest brightly: "Acapulco." When a reporter, profiling her husband, sent her a list of questions, her answers were candidly offbeat for the wife of an American politician. "What a dreary question," she wrote in answer to a query as to whether Kennedy remembered birthdays and anniversaries. Asked if he did any household chores, she replied: "Really do you think I welcome him home after ten days in West Virginia to ask him to mow the lawn?" Asked about her style of life, she countered: "How can you say this in an *unfolksy* way?" What she was trying to do, she said, was to create a private haven for her husband, "something he can find peace in," that she considered her real job.

Typically, she painted all night when her husband was nominated for President at Los Angeles, and she, pregnant, was secluded at the Cape with her mother and stepfather. Jackie alternated between her painting and the television set and finished the painting just before dawn. It was a comic portrayal of candidate Kennedy's victorious return to Hyannis.

Later, after the big campaign ticker-tape parade in New York, which taxed her energy, she put on an old raincoat and went off with William Walton, Georgetown neighbor, Kennedy volunteer and artist, to the Tibor de Nagy Gallery, a show place for the abstract. "I've looked at your kind of paintings, now come look at mine," she ordered, referring to a current exhibit of French eighteenth-century prints.

And then, suddenly, her life was transformed. Within a few weeks of her husband's victory, John, Jr., was born, and the new President-elect had a male heir. On the eve of the Inauguration, friends reported she was bubbling over with excitement and anticipation and relief—that her baby had been born safely, that the campaign ordeals were over, that she would be seeing more of her husband than in a long, long time.

First, to get back her strength for the new life, she went to Palm Beach, willowy and trim again. From there, she wired politico-artist friend Bill Walton, on learning the news he had been named Deputy Grand Marshal of the Inaugural parade. He was given to the wearing of old clothes day and night and her message was: WILL YOU WEAR BLUE JEANS A BIT TOO TIGHT YOUR TRADEMARK OR OLD CORDUROY JACKET IN WHICH YOU GREETED MRS. LA GUARDIA IN NEW YORK? Then, by mail, she further ribbed him with news that a grand surprise might be on its way to him. She had overheard Vice President-elect Lyndon Johnson say he intended to present a pregnant Hereford, a Texas rancher's highest token of esteem, to her husband. JFK's brisk response, she alleged, was: "Send it to Walton. He'll know what to do with it." A troubled Johnson then asked, "What's Walton's phone number? I want to make damn sure he's there when my cow arrives."

For Jacqueline and John Kennedy the Inauguration, January 20, 1961, despite the freezing weather, and the Inaugural-eve blizzard, was to usher in the best years of their lives. Her pride in her husband that day was touching; and the buoyant mood of this golden girl seemed to infect the nation, too. "She's going to be a supersonic first lady," predicted Mrs. John Sherman Cooper, wife of the Senator from Kentucky, "with a great sense of office and dash. The American people don't mind someone's being different if they can communicate."

The new role of First Lady did not come automatically to Jacqueline. She went to Capitol Hill to hear JFK's first address to Congress. When she appeared in the House of Representatives gallery, with a little fixed, remote smile, she was greeted by a roll of applause. It seemed to surprise her and she hesitated, as if not sure the acclaim was for her, then brushed back a forelock and gave an appealing, little-girl bow.

Betty Beale, the influential, grande dame society writer for the Washington *Star*, wrote an open letter of advice to the new First Lady. It would no longer do, wrote Miss Beale, to be a passive bystander. Now she must play an active part and promote the arts and the prestige of the nation. Mrs. Kennedy was intrigued by the article, called a friend about it, and then sent a note to Miss Beale saying she was grateful for the advice.

Jacqueline's personal little touches that were to change so the pace and style of the White House were manifested at once. The day she and JFK officially moved into the mansion, she arranged for their Georgetown portable bar to be sent over, stocked with a bottle of chilled Dom Perignon champagne for an intimate, house-warming toast.

Whether Miss Beale's advice was one persuasive factor or not, White House life did change promptly and spectacularly. For sixteen years under the Trumans and Eisenhowers the White House ambience reflected a pedestrian, elderly bonhomie. Suddenly life there appeared to crackle and sparkle. There were the late dinner dances under chandeliers, the gaggle of Kennedy cousins surging over the house and lawns, the look of youthful faces and the spouting of ideas from the artists, writers and intellectuals who invaded the place by invitation.

Within months the world was taking notice as well as the nation. Jacqueline, it appeared, was sparking as much unrest behind the Iron Curtain as a posse of CIA operatives. The Polish magazine *Swiat*, read by

restive young Poles, was smartly whacked by Communist officials for printing that Mrs. Kennedy had given a new "tone and style" for the "epochal 6o's" not only to the West, but perhaps to the entire world. The magazine lauded her for her interest in art, literature, and the theater, for her "lack of racial prejudice," for her "independent mind," and for being a new friend in court for the neglected U.S. intelligentsia. Even the "home-made, naive realism" of her paintings, it said, was influencing young Polish artists, along with the "Jackie look." And further to the Marxian East, the Soviet press, while employing meat-ax prose on JFK, called his wife "beautiful."

The Communists reflected the excited curiosity at home. That first spring tourists by the millions swarmed through Washington, hankering mostly not for a look at the familiar attractions such as the FBI, but to catch a glimpse of Jack, Jacqueline, Caroline, or John, Jr., through the high iron White House fence. The First Lady's personal tastes inspired quick, nation-wide copycatting. Plastic surgeons reported a rush of clients asking for nose bobs à la Jackie. Her "little nothing" sleeveless sheaths, which she'd worn for years, were copied into the boring tens of thousands. College girls fell to imitating her breathless, small voice. Indicating an interest never ignited by Mamie, Bess, or even Eleanor, two million copies of a paperback romance of her life were snapped up even before she began rearranging the White House furniture, and playing musical chairs with the portraits of Presidents.

Her insistence on pursuing her own feminine life style, apart from her husband's milieu of politics and statecraft, gave rise to hopes she could help liberate the Organization Wife from bondage. "She's already done more for modern women than the suffragettes," was one extravagant assessment of her; "if only by making the beautiful things that satisfy a woman's soul seem important to the rest of the world."

Just what inspired this phenomenal interest? There was always an air of mystery about her, though anecdotes began to circulate about some of her bright, offbeat quips. There was the night, for instance, when a party-loving Republican Senator, who had been fighting a Kennedy school bill, was strolling along F Street in Washington and was overtaken by a White House limousine. The car slowed down, and the First Lady leaned out. She was perched on a jump seat while the President rode the back seat. "I thought you were going to be nice to us (referring to the legislation)" she called out gaily. "If you're not, I won't let you take out Tish Baldridge any more."

She quite bowled over VIP foreigners, such as France's proud, unbending President Charles De Gaulle and Russia's dour Andrei A. Gromyko. De Gaulle, on a previous state junket, had come away impressed by two Americans, Dwight Eisenhower, and the wife of Senator Kennedy, who riveted his attention by speaking near-perfect French at a French Embassy reception. The dead-pan Gromyko, after a first grim meeting with President Kennedy, unbent and smiled only when meeting Jacqueline and Caroline.

After the Kennedys' first big party for the diplomatic corps, the long-time Peruvian Ambassador Fernando Berckemeyer declared he had "never had so much fun in the White House." His hostess, whom he had known since girlhood, greeted him with, "Aren't you going to kiss me?" One observer wrote that her animated chatting in French with the new heads of embassies from French Africa may mark "a revolution in American relations with underdeveloped countries. She may be worth more than all the military and economic aid America might send them. What people want is to be accepted, not bullied or bought."

Angier Biddle Duke, the State Department's protocol chief, found that Jackie had become the No. 1 status symbol for prospective visiting statesmen from abroad. Their first question when arrangements were being discussed was: will Mrs. Kennedy be on hand? If so, then the visitors would bring over an entourage of aunts, sisters, and mothers. In all, some seventy-three Chiefs of State came calling on the Kennedys during their tenure. When Prime Minister Eamon de Valera of Ireland arrived, Mrs. Kennedy peppered him with questions about his nieces and nephews, his family tree. When Prime Minister Jawaharlal Nehru of India settled on the White House lawn via helicopter, there was Caroline with a red rose for his buttonhole.

She was influencing the style of American diplomacy, if not the substance. When her husband insisted that, in the swapping of state presents, one gift should be distinctively made-in-America, Jacqueline came up with the design for magnificent paperweights, each unique, made of an unusual American stone and bound with gold rope. These gifts proved so successful that Konrad Adenauer, the West German chancellor, put in an advance request for one.

The Kings of Morocco and Libya, among other visitors, brought magnificently jeweled swords as mementoes. That gave her a notion: wouldn't leaders of new countries especially appreciate a replica of a sword dating from America's own revolutionary past? George Washington's battle sword perhaps?

JFK at first balked at the idea of replicas. "How would I feel," he asked, "if De Gaulle, say, gave me a copy of a Napoleonic sword? Wouldn't it seem a cheap souvenir?" Then, argued Jackie, make it the most splendid copy possible and produce it in limited edition.

Although blade drawing is virtually a vanished art in America, craftsmen were chased down in the Rock Island, Illinois, arsenal. Then the hunt was on for ivory for the handle; a U.S. military attaché in the Congo took care of that. Next problem: how to dye the ivory green. DuPont came up with a dye. The final product was the finest sword made anywhere in the last twenty-five years, and so uncannily like the original, it had to be secretly marked. Emperor Haile Selassie got the first, Ireland's de Valera the second. A third was saved for John, Jr.

Jacqueline worked with her husband on the design for a new Medal of Freedom, the only decoration, he had discovered, that a President could award distinguished civilians with no strings attached. The old medal was stark, plain, bronze, and "undistinguished," said a dissatisfied JFK; at his insistence, the Army's Institute of Heraldry was ordered to come up with a new "beautiful and fitting" design. But, studying the test striking while vacationing at Hyannis Port, neither of the Kennedys was pleased. Blue, gold, and white predominated and Jacqueline decided more red was needed. That weekend she drew sketches for a redesigned medal and ribbon, and sent them to an old friend in New York, jeweler David Webb, who had helped out with the paperweight. Webb added final touches, such as rounding the wings of the eagles to make them look less warlike. Jackie found this a "warm" rendition and at last the medal was struck.

She labored to preserve the small old houses which faced Lafayette Square, across from the White House, seeking to retain the early American flavor of the Square in the face of plans for a huge executive office building and courthouse building.

Another time she brought a newspaper story to her husband's attention. Egypt's great historic treasures, the Nubian temples on the Nile, were to be inundated and lost forever, with the building of the Aswan dam, for lack of funds to save them. Egyptologists and UNESCO had worked frantically to raise an estimated $50 million to preserve this heritage, but the U.S. government thus far had been indifferent. At this point, White House staffer Richard N. Goodwin was drafted to compile a thick document on costs and techniques for moving the temples, and JFK asked Congress to contribute millions in counterpart funds to help save the temples.

Jacqueline's unique touches did much to make the brilliant White House galas which added zip to the Washington scene. On reading that Basil Rathbone had given a recital of Elizabethan music and poetry at the Library of Congress, she listened to tapes of the performance. An invitation to Rathbone followed. At her request, he changed the repertoire for his White House appearance to include a favorite JFK Shakespeare selection— King Henry V's St. Crispin's day speech, as well as a John Donne poem for herself.

She brought a mischievous, gay and informal atmosphere to these White House parties. At her famous, glittering dinner for Nobel Prize laureates, she merrily complained to Linus Pauling, a two-time winner, that he was confusing her daughter Caroline. How? Well, she replied, he had been picketing the White House that day and Caroline, spying him, had asked: "What's daddy done wrong now?" She was inventive at entertaining. She used the lawn of historic Mount Vernon on the Potomac to fete President Ayub Khan of Pakistan at a black-tie dinner, and then took a spate of newspaper criticism about its expense and lavishness. She made sure that White House white-tie dinners had appropriate, dazzling entertainment. There was cellist Pablo Casals for Governor Luis Muñóz Marín of Puerto Rico and Metropolitan Opera stars for President Manuel Prado of Peru. With the night-time doors of the White House thrown open to the intellectual and artistic elite of the nation, a White House invitation became a status symbol.

Her specialties, however, were not the splendid soirees for honored guests nor even the late dinner dances for thirty or forty people. Rather they were the small family dinner parties, the same format she used to help her husband relax in their Georgetown years. To these exclusive dinners she would invite the President's old PT-boat buddies or Ethel and Bob and other Kennedy relatives, or legislators and government officials more interesting for their conversational flair than for their rank. Often, a couple completely outside the circle of close friends or government would be invited. A sample of the talk at these dinners was supplied by Romain Gary, the French novelist, who was invited along with future wife, Jean Seberg, to a dinner for six. Their dinner companions were the President and Mrs. Kennedy and the Richard Goodwins.

Gary was amazed at the range of subjects and by the President's habit of relentlessly questioning his guests about everything. JFK didn't converse so much as he probed. Kennedy noted that French streets were named after famous men of letters, while American streets tended toward such prosaic names as Main Street and Broadway. Why not a Hemingway Square or a Melville Boulevard, asked the President. He looked forward to the day, he said, when a kid would come home and say he had been playing baseball on "William Faulkner Avenue." JFK wanted to know whether television menaced the film industry and he pressed home scores of questions about France and Europe. Did they really believe America wanted to dominate them? Didn't they realize that the U.S. dollar depended on European prosperity? Kennedy flicked out an allusion to Albert Camus, the French writer, as he talked. He praised the Peace Corps, he spoke of his children—"To have children is the beginning of political wisdom," he said. Gary wanted to know what Kennedy would do after eight years in the White House. "You'll have a lot of time to write," said Jackie. "I'll have to hurry," retorted the President with a grin. "I'm surrounded by historians and writers who'll be rushing to get their books out ahead of mine."

If Jacqueline's tastes drastically changed the style of living in the White House, they changed the old mansion itself even more. If her knowledge of American history was not precise, at least she had a deep sense of the past and a wish to make the furnishings and decorations of the White House reflect the flow of that history and the growth of the Republic. Because of her call for forgotten pieces that had once adorned the White House and had then been moved out by successive Presidents or First Ladies, thousands of Americans began rooting through attics, barns, and antique shops for furniture that might fit the bill.

Lorraine W. Pearce, a full-time White House curator, and a Fine Arts Committee headed by Henry Francis du Pont, the creator of Delaware's prized Winterthur restoration, were put to work to redo entirely the interior of the White House on a historical motif mingled with Jackie's own feeling for warmth and elegance. American Indian prints by George Caitlin were borrowed from the Smithsonian Institution and hung in the President's private quarters. Representative volumes from the best in American history, biography, and literature were marshalled for the White House library. Five coats of paint changed the green State Dining Room to an airy antique-white and the room was filled with pieces rich in American tradition, from a George P. A. Healy portrait of President Lincoln to a flower-filled centerpiece once owned by President Monroe. The Diplomatic Reception Room was redone with 127-year-old wallpaper carrying scenes of early America and printed from wooden blocks by Jean Zuber in France. The paper had been discovered in a Maryland house about to be demolished by Peter Hill, a young lay minister. Jacqueline supervised the redecoration of the entire room. She planned to have each President represented by at least one object in the White House, but she was determined that the whole would reflect no particular occupant. While the historical refurbishing went on in the public rooms of the mansion, Mrs. Kennedy worked assiduously at bringing a bright, warm glow to the family quarters. The Oval Room fronting on Truman's balcony and overlooking the Washington monument was redone in soft yellows that had an intimate, family appearance. The President's office was refurnished with a salty, informal, man's look. Comfort was merged with eye appeal.

The whole house showed a hundred small Jacqueline touches, such as the sixty-odd paintings borrowed for the walls, the absence of stuffy reception lines, the liberal presence of ash trays, the logs burning in the fireplaces, the artfully arranged flowers that ran to such personal favorites as lilies of the valley, tulips, anemones, apple blossoms. One Republican wife was prompted to say after a tea: "I felt like a guest in the beautiful home of a gracious hostess." Then there was the excellent cuisine, prepared by a chef from France, whose importation caused great turmoil in the press. The wines, too, were a far cry from the plain ice water once served by Mrs. Warren Harding.

In due time, in the most unique public appearance by any First Lady, Jacqueline went on television in an hour-long show to guide the public via the camera's eye through the redecorated House of the Presidents. The show was such a smash success it was rerun, and provoked such intense interest that in succeeding months tourists swarmed to the White House in throngs, breaking all previous records. Jackie's performance, from the standpoint of dramatic proficiency, was charming if amateur. She was a bit wooden, and her wondering little-girl voice as she pointed out historic objects gave the political satirists fodder for months. Still, the public loved it.

Jack Kennedy once doodled on a pad to indicate the difference between himself and wife. He drew a straight, horizontal line for himself and a wavering, intersecting line for Jacqueline. "She has a very retentive memory," he said, thus marking himself as one of the few men who would list that as a leading admirable feminine trait. "She's a romantic by temperament . . ." he said, "more sensitive than my sisters who are direct and energetic. You might even call her fey."

Bobby Kennedy, the President's Attorney General and right-hand man, analyzed the First Lady this way: "She's poetic, whimsical, provocative, independent, and yet very feminine. Jackie has always kept her own identity and been different. That's important in a woman. What husband wants to come home at night and talk to another version of himself? Jack knows she'll never greet him with, 'What's new in Laos?'"

Bob's wife Ethel, the whirlwind of the Kennedy women, said of Jacqueline: "You'll have a hard time getting to the bottom of *that* barrel, which is great for Jack, who's so inquisitive. The wheels go around constantly in Jackie's head. You can't pigeon-hole her. Her house in Georgetown was such heaven and so supremely well organized. I always got depressed coming back to my madhouse."

Columnist Krock said of his old friend and now First Lady: "A Victorian wife, not the chic Long Island Piping Rock variety. A Beaux Arts type of girl, merry, arch, satirical, terribly democratic and, yes, brilliant."

A relative said flatly of Jacqueline: "She was really prepared for one eventuality in life—to be exquisite." Said an admirer who sensed her limitations: "She was born in first class and she never looked around to see who was traveling beneath her." A close friend called her "an egghead, though not of the Arthur Schlesinger variety, thank God."

Others saw her as "imaginative, offbeat," tending to poke fun at her husband when he grew too serious, or as "a great wit with a good ear for mimicry," or as a "private girl with a regal bearing, calm and serene," or as "a woman with a marvelous memory who can quote Lord Byron for five minutes straight." In a sense, all of her friends saw the same complex, introspective Jacqueline, much as they might stress differing characteristics.

The First Lady's mother one day mused about her daughter. "There's a certain stiffness about Jackie," she said, "even shyness. She was that way even with Jack for a long time. It's not that she's frightened of people, but she's not outgoing. She has marvelous self-control which perhaps conceals certain inner tensions. She has always felt very, very intensely about things. I wouldn't call her off-beat or arty, but she does have enormous individuality."

She recalled that Jackie was something of a rebel as a girl. At family lunches, French was the obligatory language, but Jackie "perversely wanted to speak German" which she'd learned from a Swiss governess. "Maybe we pushed her too far," said her mother, "and she went the other way. I always thought she had the temperament and talent of a writer, that perhaps she could write novels, poetry or fairy tales."

Jacqueline didn't do much writing as First Lady, but she did live her private life much as she had done since her marriage. She loved the outdoors and she continued to revel in it. She rode horses at their rented Virginia home, Glen Ora. She water-skiied at Palm Beach and Hyannis. She spruced up her tennis on the White House courts (to a Secret Service agent pressed to play with her one day, she confessed that she was practicing up in hopes of beating Ethel). She took golf lessons so she could play with her husband.

Where her husband read biography and history, she read *Paris Match*, Skira art books, novelists of the *avant garde*, and books about the White House. She was an avid movie buff and liked to view foreign imports in the White House projection room, although she'd watch the horse operas and spectacles enjoyed by her husband. She kept up with French literature. She could still recite "The Vision of Sir Launfal" which she'd learned as a girl of ten for her mother's birthday. And she could quote long chunks of Stephen Vincent Benet's *John Brown's Body*, which she'd learned as a bride for JFK. She kept the White House record-player spinning with French and Italian tunes and scores of Broadway musicals including a favorite, *Camelot*.

But the primary role of Mrs. Kennedy was not as fashion-setter, patroness of the arts, the private woman, or even First Lady. First and foremost she regarded herself as a mother. If she did not succeed there, she felt, she had failed throughout. Although Caroline and John, Jr., had a nanny, Maud Shaw, and there were maids, servants, and the reliable Muggsy O'Leary to look after them, it was their mother who intended to rear, guide, and discipline them.

She said after the election that she did not want her children reared by Secret Service agents and nurses. They did get attention from both, of course, but Jacqueline made sure they had plenty of motherly guidance and a raft of playmates. At the White House Caroline played constantly with her cousins, especially the children of Jean Kennedy Smith.

There was a tender, imaginative quality in the talents Mrs. Kennedy brought to child-rearing. "Let's go out and kiss the wind," she'd say to Caroline and the little girl, her eyes agleam and her imagination fired, would dash toward the bright blue ocean at Palm Beach, kissing the sea breezes. Jackie read books to her daughter in a little nook of the Palm Beach house, luring the girl by saying, "Come and play with me in our secret house."

"Maybe you can just throw away the theories when thinking about raising a child," she said. "The personality of the child seems to guide you. Children have imagination, a quality that seems to flicker out in so many adults. That's why it's such a joy to be with children."

The mother's love enveloped Caroline who in turn shared it with her baby brother whom she called "the kissing baby." Little John, to Caroline, was "my baby" and when her father, the President, called the boy "Jack," she would protest: "My baby's name isn't Jack. It's John."

Caroline had fun with her mother, whom she called "mommy." They played hide-and-seek endlessly at one period. When Jacqueline would pose for a photograph alone, Caroline would race into focus, begging to get into the picture too. Every birthday of Caroline's was celebrated by Mrs. Kennedy with a party for her daughter's friends. She was tolerant sometimes like any mother, about her offspring's behavior. When Caroline mischievously turned on a garden faucet at Palm Beach and streaked away, Jackie did not reprimand her. Once she said to a friend: "I know I should stop her from jumping in your lap, but I just can't."

Jacqueline did not leave the education of the children to others. Her mother, Mrs. Auchincloss, says she always encouraged young Jackie to do something creative for friends and relatives rather than buying them presents. "Something you create yourself is the best kind of present," she in turn told Caroline. As a result, when two and a half, Caroline drew a picture birthday card for her father.

The White House years were the happy years, not only for mother and children, but for wife and husband. For Jacqueline, the White House almost seemed like a permanent home after the many moves of her girlhood and early marriage. The little dinner parties were held several times a week, but many nights the President and Jacqueline dined alone by candlelight. She matured in her love and the President seemed to deepen in his feelings for her. For one thing, he was enormously proud of her official conduct as First Lady. For another, they grew to know each other better. There had really been so little time before. There had been periods when Kennedy would return exhausted from a delegate-wooing trip, go to bed in the Georgetown house, and leave again without more than a hurried hello and good-bye to her.

"I never had or wanted a life of my own," she said afterward. "Everything centered about Jack. I was so fiercely loyal to him. I once said thoughtlessly he should be President for life. No, he said, even if he were re-elected, eight years in the Presidency were enough for any man."

She would recite poetry for him, read his favorite prose passages aloud. Strangely, for all the pressures of the Presidency, there now seemed some leisure for the enjoyment of each other. One friend recalls a poignant scene. He had been conferring with the President and then JFK met his wife in a corridor of the White House. They joined hands and walked away, hand in hand, oblivious of servants and Secret Service agents. Jacqueline had become to John Kennedy what she had always hoped to become: his haven, his refuge, his separate world.

In the last months, particularly, they drew ever closer. The death of newborn Patrick in 1963 was a terrible blow to both of them. JFK, the taut, disciplined man, wept openly. Of five prospective children for the large family John Kennedy wanted, only two survived, and the sorrow over the losses bound husband and wife as close as did the joy over Caroline and John, Jr.

When she went on a Texas political tour in November, 1963, the hopes of the strategists soared, for one morning, radiant at the reception she and her husband were receiving, she told JFK's close friend and adviser, Larry O'Brien: "I'm going to be making a lot of these trips next year." O'Brien's Irish face glowed with delight.

A few hours later the Presidential convertible passed before the Texas School Book Depository Building in downtown Dallas—and the lights in Jacqueline Kennedy's life went out.

"I should have known that it was asking too much to dream that I might have grown old with him . . ."

On December 29, 1962, the President made a
rarely impassioned speech at the Orange Bowl in
Miami, greeting the hundreds of Cubans
taken prisoner during the luckless Bay of Pigs
landing, and newly released in exchange for
millions of dollars in medical supplies.
Mrs. Kennedy raised cheers with her little
speech in Spanish: "It is my wish and hope that
some day he [John Jr.] may be a man at least
half as brave as the members of Brigade 2506."

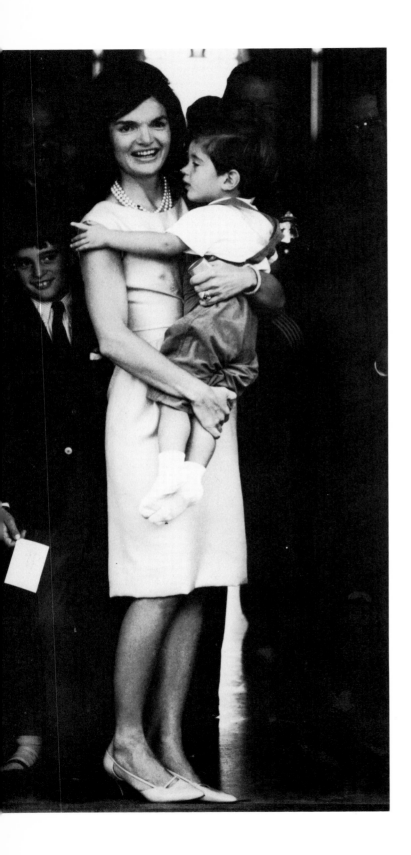

Mrs. Kennedy carried John down
the White House steps to meet Astronaut
Gordon Cooper. Her son was crazy about
anything that flew in the air, including
spacemen, and clearly anyone meeting
Junior was just as crazy about him.

Above: Jacqueline Kennedy, on that first triumphal trip to Europe, wowed Paris, Vienna, and London. Not even Nikita had ever seen a First Lady quite like her.

Right: Madame Kennedy held her own, too, with Charles De Gaulle, chatting with him in French about French literature and the theater.

Vienna, June, 1961. At that first icy summit meeting, Khrushchev and Kennedy disagreed, but their two ladies —as dissimilar as their nations—got together for a kaffee klatsch in a Vienna palace under a baroque chandelier.

Glimpses of Jacqueline Bouvier Kennedy, who, in her own style, is as complex and elusive a human as her husband ever was.

Upper left: At a children's concert on the White House lawn, 1962.
Lower left: On the way to Sunday Mass, Middleburg, 1962.
Middle: At the especially sumptuous White House reception for the Shah of Iran, 1962.
Right: On the beach at Hyannis Port, 1964.

"He is free and
we must live"

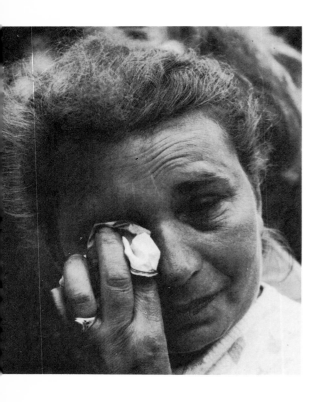

Afterward, in the long days and months when there was no John Kennedy, people could remember precisely where they were, what they were doing, and what they said when they heard the news from Dallas. The day of the telescopic rifle became, for Americans, a kind of personal Pearl Harbor, incredible, infamous, unthinkable.

But unlike Pearl Harbor, they could not rush to arms to give vent to their feelings. They could not take a war job or give up gasoline. There was little they could do, it seemed, save grieve and sorrow and feel ashamed that this thing had happened in their country. Some prayed. Almost everyone except the callous wept. For millions the sense of loss was utterly personal.

So many people, as Ted Sorensen found, felt more deeply affected about the assassination than the death of their own parents; for the latter often represented a "loss of the past," while Kennedy was an "incalculable loss of the future."

It was a strange, unique phenomenon in American life: a young, intelligent, winning, and complex President, brutally robbed of his years, instantly became the object of more admiration and affection than when he lived, and honored as he had never been in life.

And, in the words of Israel's Ben Gurion, it was the first world-wide mourning in history. For strangely enough, and this was hardly recognized on November 22, the same shock that crushed Americans was felt round the globe. In remote hamlets, huts, villages, people who had never seen John F. Kennedy reeled with the news. There were tears in black Africa, in yellow Asia, in brown India, under the hot sun of the Arab lands, and even in the Communist countries. In Latin America they said special masses in the churches, illiterate Indian women lamented the fallen American President as if they mourned a beloved member of the family. "He was really our President, too," said a young Arab shiek. "What I admired especially was his bravery over Cuba, but more than that, I felt he was of my own generation."

The reaction in other lands had little to do with politics. For the humble and poor of the earth, it was another promise gone, another page torn from life's book of ever-fraying hopes. A glowing, confident young man of so much unfulfilled promise had been cut down in the sunlight of life. To many, his going symbolized the senseless, irrational world in which they found themselves. Only a political-psychiatrist could analyze why, when, and how President Kennedy had gotten into the sinews and bloodstreams of hundreds of millions of humble people around the globe, but his death proved, to an astonishing degree, that he had.

In the United States the four days of televised mourning and funeral ground forward like the relentless playing of a Greek tragedy. The incessant roll of the funeral drums throbbed in the body like an evil drug, and men who hadn't cried in years found themselves weeping again and again. The shame of the killing, the preposterous illogic, the irrelevance, the caprice, and tragedy of human life, all these feelings swelled the agony. And yet, again for Americans, there was a source of wondering pride in the hours and days before the burial and the lighting of the eternal flame in Arlington National Cemetery. The source was a woman, a beautiful, fiercely noble woman in black.

Jacqueline Kennedy walked through the ceremonies of death like a monarch who'd lost a war, but not an empire. She walked with grandeur in her marriage, her eyes straight and unwavering, her poise almost glacial. No heroine of the stage ever played a tragic part to such perfection. Gone was the shy, elusive, sylvan creature who sometimes appeared too ephemeral for this world. Now unexpected steel showed from deep within her, and she marched with the resolute tread of the pioneer women who had followed the covered wagons across the plains.

"My wife is a very strong woman," President Kennedy had said once, but the nation had no clue to it then. Her actions after November 22, 1963, were more than the "mechanical compliance" that people make in appalling circumstances, wrote Mary McGrory in the Washington *Evening Star*. "It has been as though she were trying to show the world that courtesy and courage did not die in Dallas."

From the outset, after the first blood-stained shock in the Dallas hospital, Jacqueline had been another chapter in her husband's *Profiles in Courage*. Flying back to Washington with the body in *Air Force One*, she sat dry-eyed while others cried. She sat with Presidential Assistants Lawrence O'Brien, Kenneth O'Donnell, and Dave Powers, the Massachusetts politicians who had devoted their lives to her husband. "What's to become of you all?" she wondered. "What are you going to do?" "We were supposed to be the tough pols," O'Brien said later, "but this frail girl turned out to have more strength than any of us." O'Brien, trying not to go to pieces, would look at Jackie's strained composure when he found himself faltering.

In that cold night vigil with the body in Bethesda Naval Hospital, she defiantly refused to change her stained pink suit. "It's his blood," she said. Then she implored Mrs. Evelyn Lincoln, his secretary, to leave. "It's getting late," she said, "and I'm going to be here quite a while, so why don't you go home and try to get some rest?"

Jacqueline's strength and that of Robert Kennedy infused the whole Kennedy clan and none broke down in public throughout the long ordeal, from the crack of the first shot to the lowering of the casket into the earth at Arlington. Robert wept alone that first day during solitary walks at his McLean country home and he donned dark glasses to hide his red-rimmed eyes. Sargent Shriver, who supervised the removal of JFK's effects from the Presidential office, cried for five minutes after the rocking chair was taken out, but he too was alone, and he dried his eyes before facing the White House staff.

They walked in a solid phalanx behind the caisson and its burden on the day of the funeral, the Kennedy men enclosing the black-veiled widow inside an apprehensive chain of Secret Service agents. As much as a tribute to the fallen leader, it was a testament to the nation that courage, composure, and dignity lived on and would not be shattered by a psychopath's bullets.

That evening, after she had received the mighty of the world in the all-day trial, Jacqueline finished her public role and then, at 6:15 P.M., she called Dave Powers. It was the third birthday of John, Jr., and since there could be no party, would Powers come up and play with the boy? They played soldiers, marching about the room and saluting, the boy first with the flag, Dave in the rear with a Presidential sword.

Jackie supervised every small detail of the vast state funeral and the leave-taking from the White House. Then two weeks almost to the hour, after the unthinkable event in Dallas, Jacqueline Kennedy, clasping the hands of her children, quietly left the White House, and that somehow was the bleakest day of all. A little truck passed through the gate bearing a bird cage, a model ship, toys, the last of family belongings.

Her departure wrote finis to the heady Kennedy era that had percolated excitement through Washington for 1,036 days, and was already cruelly receding in memory. To the last, she made sure her husband's era would end with grace. She bade personal good-byes to the White House staff, then walked over to the Executive Office Building for a thank-you farewell to the phone operators; she left a bouquet and a note for the new First Lady, Mrs. Lyndon Johnson; to the few people who had shared John F. Kennedy's brief White House years, she gave mementos: Mrs. Lincoln wept again when she got hers—two flags, U.S. and Presidential, that had graced the Oval Office. She remembered even White House photographer, Cecil Stoughton, who had taken so many happy pictures for the family album; to him she sent one of the President's ties. She asked the Attorney General to phone the widow of police officer J. D. Tippitt, who had been killed in the Dallas nightmare.

That Friday, leaving the White House she was no longer the tragic heroine, regal and pathetic, whom the world had watched bear senseless sorrow with almost superhuman dignity, but a young widow, with two small children, alone with memory, yet with a new life to begin. At first, she wanted to live in "all the places Jack lived," she said, and that meant Georgetown. Old friend Franklin D. Roosevelt, Jr., dropping in like so many old friends, found "she makes it easy to talk about the President. She wants to hear everything about him. I think she realized fully from the first what had happened, absorbing the reality—sooner than most of us could."

But there were the awful days too, the abysses of despair when she felt she couldn't go on. "How do you keep going?" she'd ask helplessly. There was unknowing John heedlessly chattering about "Daddy's plane." Of the children, it was Caroline at an age to remember, who was most deeply hurt and became a "changed child," withdrawn at times, shy, quiet, moody. Only Uncle Bobby could coax her out of her shell. She would whisper to him the confidences she had once poured into the ear of her father. Robert Kennedy treated the children with infinite tenderness.

The brother's sorrow seemed bottomless. Tragedy had stalked the family as though it were fated. First his oldest brother, Joe, had been killed in World War II. His sister Kathleen had died in an air crash. Then a stroke crippled his father. Then an assassin shot his cherished brother, Jack. And, in a few months, his younger brother, Senator Ted Kennedy, almost died, breaking his back in the crash of a small plane. Bob Kennedy spent as much time as he could with Jacqueline's children, at Hyannis, in Washington, at his own home in Virginia. And he tried to comfort Jackie. He would stroll in the country with her, clasping her hand as though to reaffirm the strength she showed in the first days.

But black moods of despair fell upon her. Her own life was over, she felt at first, and her only job was to get through one day after another until the children were grown. Once she thought of turning the children over to Bobby, for she felt her agony must be infecting them. She was, she felt, little more than "a living wound." He told her no, she must go on. She abhorred the thought of Dallas and Texas and once she said she would never go back to the state. Guns tormented her and she forbade John, Jr., to play with them, although, like most boys, he loved the bang-bang games. Once she grabbed a gun from him and scolded: "I told you I don't want any guns in here."

Everything seemed to be a reminder of the radiant, handsome young President. The Army sent her the trappings of the riderless horse that had followed the caisson bearing her husband's body down Pennsylvania Avenue—saber, boots, blanket, and bridle. Hundreds of thousands of letters of condolence poured in, and ten volunteers were mustered to handle them. In the summer, she went back to Hyannis, but the boom of the surf, the fog over the shamrock-green lawns, the bright cackle of the little cousins, all reminded her of Jack. And always around her were the Secret Service men, under special act of Congress, as a symbol of the Presidency and the husband who held it. She had gone back to the Cape to be with her husband's close-knit family, and because for her children in a year of

199

change, it was an oasis of normality. But here memory was a trap. There from the breakwater was the sea view JFK had loved best as boy and man; and in the waves bobbed a little boat christened PT Boat 109½.

That fall, for a Kennedy memorial issue of *Look* magazine, she wrote poignantly of her husband and the months since Dallas. Usually she wrote easily, she said, but she wrote draft after draft of her personal tribute, trying to say what was almost unsayable.

"It is nearly a year since he has been gone.

"On so many days—his birthday, an anniversary, watching his children running to the sea—I have thought, 'But this day last year was his last to see that.' He was so full of love and life on all those days. He seems so vulnerable now, when you think that each one was a last time.

"Soon the final day will come around again—as inexorably as it did last year. But expected this time.

"It will find some of us different people than we were a year ago. Learning to accept what was unthinkable when he was alive changes you.

"I don't think there is any consolation. What was lost cannot be replaced.

"Someone who loved President Kennedy, but who had never known him, wrote to me this winter: 'The hero comes when he is needed. When our belief gets pale and weak, there comes a man out of that need who is shining—and everyone living reflects a little of that light—and stores up some against the time when he is gone.'

"Now I think that I should have known that he was magic all along. I did know it—but I should have guessed that it could not last. I should have known that it was asking too much to dream that I might have grown old with him and see our children grow up together.

"So now he is a legend when he would have preferred to be a man. I must believe that he does not share our suffering now. I think for him—at least he will never know whatever sadness might have lain ahead. He knew such a share of it in his life that it always made you happy whenever you saw him enjoying himself. But now he will never know more—not age, nor stagnation, nor despair, nor crippling illness, nor loss of any more people he loved. His high noon kept all the freshness of the morning—and he died then, never knowing disillusionment.

'. . . he has gone . . .
Among the radiant, ever venturing on,
Somewhere, with morning, as such spirits will.'

"He is free and we must live. Those who love him must know that 'the death you have dealt is more than the death which has swallowed you.'"

For that memorial issue she wrote in long-hand her comments on the

200

authors and works that Kennedy most admired. There were Tennyson's poem "Ulysses," a passage from which she had memorized for him; lines from Shakespeare's *King Richard III* and *King Henry V;* Pericles' funeral oration for Greeks who died in battle; Robert Frost; Benét's *John Brown's Body;* Thomas Davis's lament for the death of Owen Roe O'Neill, an Irish rebel patriot.

Reflected in them, she felt, were so many John F. Kennedys—the man of action, hungry for life; the man preoccupied with restoring politics as an honorable profession; and, unexpectedly, the man, notably disciplined in public, with a private streak of romanticism and attraction to lost causes, haunted, too, by the poignancy of men dying young.

His favorite book, she recalled, was *Pilgrim's Way,* the memoirs of John Buchan, Lord Tweedsmuir, especially Buchan's portrait of Raymond Asquith, brilliant eldest son of a British Prime Minister. Raymond Asquith died early, killed in action in World War I. Jackie in her firm hand copied lines from the portrait that seemed to capture her own husband as well. "You see," she wrote in a personal comment, "how alike they were and how strange it is he would admire a man—with awe almost—in his young days and end up being so like him." She copied these lines:

"But for the chosen few, like Raymond, there is no disillusionment. They march on into life with a boyish grace, and their high noon keeps all the freshness of the morning. Certainly to his cradle the good fairies brought every dower. They gave him great beauty of person; the gift of winning speech; a mind that mastered readily whatever it cared to master; poetry and the love of all beautiful things; a magic to draw friends to him; a heart as tender as it was brave. Only one gift was withheld from him—length of years."

Jacqueline rephrased one sentence of this in her own memorial to her husband, for Buchan's statement, lyrically phrased, that in some persons, "their high noon keeps all the freshness of the morning," had become a part of her now.

Her mood was one of sad longing when I talked to her in Hyannis that first summer after the assassination. "I try not to be bitter," she said then, aware that she still felt that emotion—that he who was so unvindictive toward his opponents could inspire such hatred—that she couldn't have borne more children for him . . . that the world, while remembering, tended to think of him as an "atypical" American, as if an American politico could not be civilized and literate. "I never had or wanted a life of my own," she said. "Everything centered around Jack. I can't believe that I'll never see him again. Sometimes I wake in the morning, eager to tell him something and he's not there. . . . Nearly every religion teaches there's an afterlife, and I cling to that hope. Those three years we spent in the

White House were really the happiest time for us, the closest, and now it's all gone. Now there is nothing, nothing." She had always looked forward to the day when, out of the White House, they could live a more human, less jet-speed life, yet now she missed the very pace he set, the excitement he brought to everything, the ability he had to spark even her, his wife, into doing her most excellent best.

As the months fell away, the brave front she had presented in public would crumble and often she'd cry. Then Caroline would try to comfort her, saying, "You're crying about Daddy, aren't you?" There were moods of depression, brought on by a small event that reminded her of the happiest years in the White House. But then she would rally and become her old self. Once she even played touch football with the Kennedys at Hyannis, the first time she had played the game since she had injured her foot as a bride.

Time slowly eased the grief. At first, she could not look at pictures of him, those were the hardest to bear, but later she showed many of the albums to the children. She worried about history's picture of him, and hoped that because of the growing martyr legend, he would not become an artificial, remote, marble-like figure, a fate she believed had befallen George Washington. She hoped he survived the years more as the vivid Thomas Jefferson. In his wide range of tastes and interests, she thought JFK much resembled Jefferson.

She left Washington, the city so flooded with memories, and took the children to live in New York, the city of anonymity. Now, the stately days of office and ceremony were behind her. She was a young widow, trying to start life afresh with the two children. She made a few new friends and when the old friends called, they found facets of the old Jackie—the sly wit, the whimsy, the joy in music, clothes, and art, the old interest in people and their doings. And then, at times, a veil would lower, and the wide-set eyes would stare, searching the distance.

Things would never be the same. . . .

All around the world the memory of John Fitzgerald Kennedy impelled men, in their own ways, to let others know the bleakness they felt. There were, of course, the standard memorials to invest his name with some kind of permanence, the bridges, the airports, the avenues, boulevards, and expressways, the half-dollars, the stamps, the buildings, the statues, the parks, the endowments, and the libraries.

But there were other memorials, highly personal, from the humble people of the world. In a far mountain village of Peru, an Indian couple hung a picture of President and Mrs. Kennedy in their home as though it were a shrine. On the island of Cozumel, off the coast of Yucatan, a Mexican woodcutter cleared an acre of tangled brush and erected a crude sign, "President Kennedy Memorial Garden." In the Dominican Republic, in a time of bloody civil war, volunteers of the U.S. Peace Corps, a Kennedy creation, freely ministered to the sick and wounded of both sides and were blessed as the "children of Kennedy." Many young men and women reacted as did Nicholas Stroh, a reporter on the *Detroit News*. "After that day in Dallas," he said, "I just felt I had to do something for the country." He joined the Peace Corps.

In Ireland, Kennedy-worship became a cult and his picture was widely sold in triptychs between those of Popes John and Paul. In Communist but Catholic Poland, the memory of the American President was so cherished that Poles mobbed his visiting brother, Robert Kennedy.

The magnetism of Kennedy, in death, was a source of wonder everywhere, but it was particularly keen in Africa. When news came of the assassination, all government offices and businesses promptly closed in a number of the new African nations. Kennedy had welcomed many African leaders to the White House and he had directed new government energies toward the continent, but it was more than that. Africa is young in self-government, young in independence. Its people are young too, for disease cuts many of them off before middle age. Africans felt a special link with the youthful American President.

More than a year after the assassination, a Peace Corps volunteer in Liberia, Patrick Galvin, a slight, curly-haired graduate of Iona College, made a trek by jeep more than 300 miles from the capital, Monrovia, to the mud-hut village of Bolahun in the high bush jungle. He took along a movie projector and a number of U.S. Information Agency films, including a documentary on JFK as candidate and President. One night 350 members of the Loma tribe gathered in a Catholic mission school to see the movie. Only a handful could speak any English and none of them had ever seen a movie or a television screen. They sat in blank silence when they saw a number of prominent Americans, but when Kennedy's face first appeared on the screen, they burst into excited cheering. "Hero! Hero!" they cried in Loma. They repeated the uproar each time Kennedy's features reappeared. Galvin was astonished. By what alchemy had the Kennedy personality penetrated this isolated town in the high African bush?

The diplomats would dissect Kennedy's statecraft, its blunders and its triumphs, from the Bay of Pigs to the nuclear test-ban treaty. The professors would analyze his speeches. The economists would weigh his impact on the forces of business and finance. The historians would assess his New Frontier in the light of the decades to come.

But the people, along with John Buchan and Jacqueline, would remember:

His high noon kept the freshness of the morning.

It is nearly a year since he has been gone. On so many days — his birthday, an anniversary, his children running to the sea, I have thought "But this day last year was his last day to see that." He was so full of love and life on al those days. He seems so vulnerable now, when you think that each one of those days was the last.

Soon the final day will come around again - as inexorably as it did last year. But expected this time.

It will find some of us different people than we were a year ago.

I dont think there is any consolation. What was lost cannot be replaced.

Someone who loved President Kennedy, but who had never known him wrote to me this winter - "The hero comes when he is needed. When our belief gets pale and weak, there comes a man out of that need who is shining, — and everyone living reflects a little of that light — and stores some up against the time when he is gone."

Now I think that I should have known that he was magic all along. I did know it — but I should have guessed that it would be too much to ask to grow old with him and see our children grow up together.

So now he is a legend when he would have preferred to be a man.

I must believe that he does not share our
suffering now. I think for him — at least he will
never know whatever sadness might have lain
ahead. He knew such a share of it in his life
that it always made you so happy whenever you
saw him enjoying himself. But now he will never
know more — not age nor stagnation nor despair,
nor crippling illness nor loss of any more people
he loved. His high noon kept all the freshness of
the morning - and he died then, never knowing
disillusionment.

"~~Ha~~..." "....he has gone
       Among the radiant, ever venturing on,
       Somewhere, with morning, as such spirits will."

He is free and we must live. Those who love him most
know that "the death you have dealt is more than
the death which has swallowed you."

For Stanley Tretick — whose pictures will always revive our most precious memories
of President Kennedy —
With love from Caroline and John and me.
Jacqueline Kennedy

Hyannis Port revisited, summer of 1964.
Barefoot and in Capri pants, she looked
like any young mother keeping a watchful
eye on her children by the sea. It was
Mrs. Jacqueline Kennedy, back at the place
her husband loved most as boy and man.
She went because she wanted to be with her
husband's closeknit family, to take her
children to a familiar place after months
of disruption and change.

That summer John, then three, was his ebullient self, but it was Caroline— of an age to remember—who was most withdrawn and troubled. Uncle Bobby could coax her out of her shell.

There was now something special between Caroline and Uncle Bobby; in him she confided the things she used to tell father.

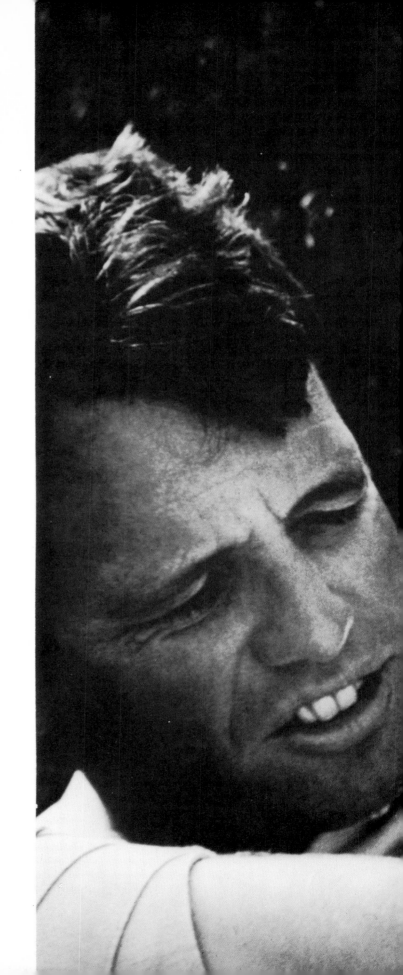

John rang up Santa Claus on the Secret Service walkie-talkie and gave a rundown on Christmas present requests— more and more airplanes, with a P.S. not to forget Caroline.

John raced up the beach with a news bulletin for his mother,
Uncle Bobby, and visiting Ted Sorensen and his wife Sally.